THINKING ABOUT THINKING

America's Yeomanry and Cognoscenti

Thomas Christ

DEFIANCE PRESS
& PUBLISHING

THINKING ABOUT THINKING

DEFIANCE **PRESS**
& PUBLISHING

ISBN-13: 978-1-959677-60-4 (Paperback)
ISBN-13: 978-1-959677-59-8 (eBook)

Published by Defiance Press & Publishing, LLC

Bulk orders of this book may be obtained by contacting Defiance Press & Publishing, LLC. www.defiancepress.com.

Public Relations Dept. – Defiance Press & Publishing, LLC
281-581-9300
pr@defiancepress.com

Defiance Press & Publishing, LLC
281-581-9300
info@defiancepress.com

Section Three: TWO REMAINING PROBLEMS

LIST OF FIGURES

LIST OF ILLUSTRATIONS

PREFACE

ANY BOOK TELLS A STORY, sometimes multiple stories, but at least one. Clearly a novel tells a story, and that story has been conjured from the mind of its author, from his or her experience as refracted by their imagination. A biography or autobiography tells the story of a life and how the man or woman who lived that life encountered the world around them. And, in every case—if most clearly in the case of the autobiography—the story reflects and incorporates something of the author: the story would be different had it been penned by a different author. Even an anthology of short stories or poems reflects the taste and judgment of its editor.

Even in the case of highly technical subjects, the story told by a book incorporates something of the author: A textbook on electronic engineering authored by one professor of engineering will differ from another such textbook authored by another professor. The choices of points of emphasis will be different; the voice of the authors will be different, on and on. The stories told about, say, geometrodynamics—the conceptualization of the universe as geometry—written by two different theoretical physicists will differ in both style and substance. Authors compose and communicate stories, and authors matter for stories.

This book tells such a story. The story is about the political division—the ideological division between Left and Right in the United States in the second decade of the twenty-first century as this book is being written—and, and this is critical, *why* this division came to exist. Our story is, thus, a story about a technical subject; it is an analytical and explanatory account of a social topic. It is, accordingly, a work of sociology. This ends up being a rather long story—and a story which takes a while to get to its ultimate topic—because it is analytic and explanatory. Finally, to say that it is "analytic and explanatory" means that it creates a *theory*, a set of ideas which purports to account for why things are as they are, and which can be used to predict and explain *other* things.

And we are ambitiously theoretical! We intend to explain people's political thinking—their ideologies—in terms, ultimately, of technology. Particular technology leads to particular ways of thinking? That sounds like a long stretch ... and it is, but if you go step by step, as we do, applying reason and evidence at each step, you end up with a theory which accounts for people's thinking in terms of material—techno-economic—reality.

And what good is that? Well, for one thing, if you know the sources of a problem—and the political divisions between Left and Right now in this country are a big problem—then you have some ability to craft approaches to resolving the problem.

More fundamentally than that, though, more fundamentally than the capacity to craft fixes for problems, an effective theory possesses its own austere aesthetic grace. To be able to read a news story and say to yourself, "Ah! I understand!" is an extraordinarily satisfying sensation. We humans are all creatures of the mind. We are built to understand. We are best when we understand our own world. "Eureka!" ("I have found it!") Archimedes is said to have cried out upon coming to understand his famous principle relating weight, buoyancy, and displacement. This satisfaction of curiosity is the human condition at its best.

In most stories, the protagonist encounters some challenges. If one intends to explain what people think in terms of techno-economic reality—material reality—one must delve into the deepest reaches of sociological theory, and that can be a tough slog. This delving will require the incorporation and integration of the social thinking of, particularly, Karl Marx, Peter Berger, Karl Mannheim, and David Riesman. These are men—Marx and Mannheim were German; Berger was Austrian-born; Riesman an American—of the late nineteenth and early and mid-twentieth centuries, and their styles of writing (and choices of topic) are not those of the twenty-first century. This author has endeavored to render these sometimes-abstruse ideas more accessible principally through the use of modern examples, but it's still not *Dick and Jane*.

This takes some time, and it takes some effort: it's not for sissies … but our readers aren't sissies!

> The shades of night were falling fast.
> As through an Alpine village passed
> A youth, who bore, 'mid snow and ice,
> A banner with the strange device,
> Excelsior!
>
> –Henry Wadsworth Longfellow

We began by saying that every book is a story and that every book contains something of the author. This author invites the reader now to come to understand—and to share—this usefully elegant way of thinking. And a new way of thinking that makes sense of a very confusing world can be enormously satisfying.

So, why do you want to read this book? Reading a book represents a substantial investment of time and attention—not to mention a bit of money—by the reader; so, what should the reader expect by way of return on that investment? It's a fair—indeed, a very important—question for any potential reader to ask of any book, and the author is obliged to provide a good answer. The potential reader of this book can expect to come away from the book with a theoretical framework—*a way of thinking*—which will enable him or her to understand the political ideological divide which separates Americans today, to understand that this ideological divide reflects a social divide, and to understand how this social divide grew out of technological and economic changes during the late twentieth and early twenty-first centuries. The way of thinking is key because you know a lot about the divisions between Right and Left, between—for example—Republican and Democrat, already. What the book will provide you is an intellectually comprehensive way of thinking about and inter-relating facts, many of which you already know.

Now, it may be that the reader is being assigned this book as required reading in some course of study. If this is the case, we would first applaud your instructor in his or her perspicacity in choice of course materials. We would note, too, that because the instructor will most likely know more about an area of study than will the student, your instructor has determined in his or her wisdom that the points of understanding in the prior paragraph will be useful for the pursuit of this course of study and that the reader's time will be well-spent.

To assert that one is going to think about thinking threatens a forced march through the most tortuous paths of academic epistemology, the part of philosophy dealing with the sources and validity of knowledge. This book intends to be nothing of the sort. It is, first of all, intended for a popular rather than—or in addition to—an academic audience in both its style and in its structure. Citations are minimized, as is the use of professional and academic jargon.

As to epistemology—the theory of knowledge, including its origin, methodology and validity—this book will necessarily rely on academic contributions to the study of knowledge because the subject of this book is contemporary ideologies and their provenance. We will strive, however, to illustrate any epistemological assertion with abundant examples that will be familiar to the contemporary reader.

The principal purposes of this book are three:

- To create a theory of ideology,

- To apply this theory to the contemporary political situation in the United States—and the widely recognized division in the American electorate and politically engaged population—such that a theoretical basis, a *way* of thinking, may be created for the understanding of that division,

- To apply the understanding thus created to that division such that the problems associated with the division might be moderated. This is, one might say, not so much social science as it is social technology.

The sort of social science upon which we will principally rely is called the "sociology of knowledge," a direct, if a bit misleading, translation of its German name: *Wissensociologie* ... and, indeed, most of the early work in the field was done in the late nineteenth century and early twentieth century by German social scientists. Section One of this volume will provide an introduction to the sociology of knowledge.

The essential—the core—notion of the sociology of knowledge is that the social situation of an individual powerfully influences their thinking. Their *thinking*. Now, is all thinking what we would currently call "knowledge?" No, and perhaps the field ought to have been translated into English as "the sociology of thinking," or "the sociology of belief"—indeed, that's closer to what *Wissen* connotes in German—but it wasn't either one of those two translations.

Moreover, the focus of the sociology of knowledge has, historically, been not upon what we would normally call "knowledge"—say, scientific knowledge or mathematical knowledge—but upon other beliefs, and, in particular, ideology. Indeed, there is a sociology of science, and its history and intellectual antecedents are very different from those of the sociology of knowledge.

The focus of this book will be ideology. As with everything, ideology has been defined multiple ways. For our purposes—as for most—ideology shall mean a belief, a system of beliefs, or a related collection of beliefs which is associated with a particular and identifiable group of people. And these beliefs are often—indeed typically—understood to be of a "non-technical" nature to distinguish them from the very specific beliefs associated with very specific social roles: a physicist has beliefs about physics; a plumber has beliefs about plumbing ... and physicists and plumbers are particular and identifiable groups of people, but such technical knowledge is not understood to constitute ideology. Our definition of ideology will be challenged by some; for instance, in recent years science itself has been labeled ideological by some writers because of its association with certain social groups.

For our purposes, then, ideological beliefs are beliefs about "softer" topics: they are political, moral, and ethical. They are topics about which anyone—not just a specialist like a physicist or plumber—can have a point of view. And if, in a society, these points of view differ by social group, they may be said to be ideological. Now, even in specialized occupations there can be differing points of view about the best way of thinking about the technical issues of their bailiwicks—and you ought to hear a physicist who is a critic of string theory go off on that point of view ("If you can't test hypotheses it's simply not science!")—but our focus will not be on such esoteric matters.

The reader might, at this point, exclaim, "Well, of course people in different groups will believe different things! People will believe what's in their own self-interest!" In fact, this is very frequently not correct. People often believe things that are bad for themselves and their families, and this will be an important focus of concern in the following pages.

This book is being written in the period following the November 2020 United States presidential election in which Joseph Biden defeated the incumbent Donald Trump by an Electoral College margin of 306 to 232 and a national popular vote margin of approximately eighty-one (51 percent) million to seventy-four (47 percent) million. In losing, President Trump gained over 11 million more popular votes relative to his 2016 winning performance. In a glib and, frankly, misleading sense, this book is mostly about the people who voted for Trump and those who voted for his Democratic competitors in 2016 and 2020.

Section One of *Thinking About Thinking* creates a "Theory of Ideology." Sections Two and Three are written with a mind to, first, understand and, second, help to ameliorate the ideological divide which plagues American politics in the early twenty-first century. We have named the two sides of this ideological divide the "yeomanry"—roughly speaking, the portion of the population which lives and works *outside* of formal organizations (think "bureaucracy"), and which supported and supports former president Donald Trump—and the "cognoscenti:" roughly the portion of the population which lives and works *inside* of formal organizations, and which opposed and opposes him. We have tried to provide an even-handed treatment to both the yeomanry and the cognoscenti: our purpose is—at least, in the analytic phases of what we argue—much more to understand than to correct or chastise. We have not attempted to disguise our displeasure with Mr. Trump as a man and as a president, but we regard him as being much more a disagreeable symptom rather than a disagreeable cause. And, while their attitudes toward Trump typify the yeomanry and the cognoscenti, *they do not define them*: more on that later.

This book—like Mr. Trump himself—is a symptom of our time and of the forces which have brought the yeomanry and the cognoscenti into conflict with one another in our time.

Now, we are not writing about political parties nor about partisanship as it is typically understood. We are writing about ideologies and about the social bases of ideologies: about how particular ideologies develop within and characterize particular social groups. That said, one of the prominent ways in which ideologies come to be expressed is in partisan affiliation. Accordingly, we will cite party affiliation at various points in our arguments, and it will be with reference to its being an expression of ideological posture and of social sector affiliation. Accordingly, there is much here which will be of relevance for understanding contemporary American partisan politics.

Much ink has been spilt in discussions of the extraordinarily deep and bitter level of political polarization in the United States in the opening decades of the twenty-first century. It has been cast in a military metaphor: "The Culture War." The metaphor is apt: the division is deep, and lines of cleavage coincide—crystalize—along partisan, occupational, geographic, and cultural-choice divides. We intend to offer an argument which will account for these cleavages and their ideological consequences.

We will also offer—at the end of our analysis in Section Three of the book—some suggestions as to how this divide might be ameliorated, and these suggestions will include efforts which are at least tangentially political. Our conception of the role of the political institution in any society is almost completely amoral: the political institution exists to peacefully adjust incompatible sets of interests and beliefs. The only normative element in this conception of the political institution is that peace is better than violence. The American Civil War—any civil war— represents a failure of the political institution. We hope that this volume might contribute to a political resolution of the current divide.

In Section Three we advocate for—specifically as a means of achieving a long-term civil discourse between the yeomanry and the cognoscenti—broad institutional changes to promote a shared, evidence-based, rational way of thinking—a "scientific" way of thinking—for both the yeomanry and the cognoscenti. We are, thus, committed to a scientific way of thinking both as a political palliative and, as well, the way in which we approach our own subject. In this latter regard, we have tried to cite evidence whenever available to support of our assertions. In a topical area as broad as thinking about thinking, evidence has not always been available. These gaps remain as potential hypotheses for testing to determine the robustness of our theory of ideology.

In sum, we are advancing a way of thinking about ideological thinking in our time. It is our hope that, by the end of this book, the reader will come away with a theoretical framework—a model—which will aid him or her in understanding what they read in the newspapers or see on news programs. Put another way, we hope to provide a framework to organize and make sense of facts that you already know.

At its best, a way of thinking will become a key that can be inserted into the lock of reality ... and turn.

Finally, and on a grammatical note, we will be using the terms "yeomanry" and "cognoscenti" more, perhaps, than any other nouns in the

English language. We understand these to be singular collective nouns. Hence, to achieve agreement in number, one would always use them as singular. We haven't done that, using them as singular or plural as has seemed to suit the sentence. This has put our MS WORD grammar checker into a deep, passive-aggressive funk. We hope that the reader will, by contrast, approve.

SECTION ONE:

A SOCIOLOGY OF IDEOLOGY

I. INTRODUCTION

THE FOCUS OF THIS BOOK is ideology, including the articulation of a theory of why different people believe as they do. This is an enormous topic—even as we have restricted it historically and geo-culturally to the United States at the beginning of the third millennium—and serious scholars have devoted major portions of their careers to the understanding of ideology. This book organizes the thinking of certain of these scholars into a theoretical framework suitable for our topic and applies this theoretical framework to our current circumstances in the United States almost a quarter of the way through the twenty-first century.

That the book endeavors to explain why some groups of people think as they do is, by itself, a substantial pretext for its existence. There is, however, a more personal basis. Optimally (and if the author has done a workmanlike job), the reader can locate both himself or herself—as well as groups of people which loom large in their lives—in this analysis and identify the analytical categories into which they fall and the ideological forces that the analysis says should be playing upon them. This sort of self-knowledge is a good thing in general, but even more of a good thing in this arena than generally. Some of the forces which impel the members of a group to believe as they do reflect the real interests and perspectives of these individual members ... and to believe something that is in one's own interest or expressive of one's perspective is, arguably, a good thing: a true consciousness. On the other hand, some social forces impel individuals to believe things which are either untrue and/or not in the interest of nor expressive of the perspective of these individuals and their loved ones. This is typically a bad thing. In our era of powerful electronic mass media and highly sophisticated marketing technique, what had been a quaint and localized error can burgeon into mass self-deception. A thinking individual's failure to comprehend the forces propelling him or her and those like him or her into a particular ideological position has been given a name by the intellectual tradition from which this book is written, the tradition called the "sociology of knowledge." It is said that those who do not have such understanding are possessed of a "false consciousness," and to be so possessed is always and ever a bad thing. The exorcism of such a false consciousness is the book's additional and more personal justification.

This book is not specifically intended to be a primarily scholarly work; it is, rather, directed at informed and thoughtful lay readers concerned about the state of contemporary American political discourse and interested in understanding how the thinking behind that discourse arises, why the various points of view have a predictable distribution among particular social groups, and what might be the current and future consequences of our fellow citizens being exposed to the ideological forces currently prevailing. To say that this is not a "scholarly" work means certain things, points which may have more meaning for academic readers than for lay readers and that consist, for the most part, in the following characteristics:

- We have tried to minimize citation. The practice of citation and attribution is an important part of scholarly writing not only because it allows for verification of sources but also because it helps scholars—who are professionally familiar with the theoretical underpinnings and antecedents of an argument—to understand how the argument which they are reading articulates with these underpinnings and antecedents. The lay reader will, however, find voluminous citation to be disruptive of the rhetorical flow of an argument and generally irrelevant for its understanding. We will discuss, in the following chapter, the principal intellectual sources of the argument we are advancing and employ our best judgment on behalf of the reader in citing sources in the book. One use of such citation is directing the interested reader to more extended discussions of points.

- We have minimized the use of prose typical to the social sciences generally and to sociology in particular. This has two dimensions: first, we have avoided, when possible (and it has not always been possible), the use of social-science jargon. Happily, not much is thereby lost. All of the sciences—and other fields, as well—employ "jargon" or "terms of art:" words unique to the field or words with a usage or meaning in a particular field which is different from that word's usage or meaning in popular English. In general, the justification for such non-conventional words or usages is that the term describes an object (a thing, process, idea, etc.), that is not adequately describable by a term or phrase from common literate English. When a physicist refers to a "muon," he or she is referring to something that is not summarily describable by common English words. Sociology has incorporated the penchant for jargon of the natural and physical sciences without bringing with it their theoretical coherence and sophistication. These two features of contemporary sociology are likely related: because the power of sociological theory is relatively weak, a term's utility is likely limited to application in a relatively few situations, and the next person who studies even those situations will likely employ a somewhat different theoretical construction, so new terms will be needed. Considering the modest increase in sophistication brought by these unfamiliar and sometimes ugly-as-home-made-sin words, we have sought to avoid their use. Second, we have tried to present the ideas to follow in a style which is reasonably lucid and accessible to the lay reader. The prose style typical to academic sociology (which is, for the most part, the only kind of sociology) is unspeakably wretched. Even sociologists hate it, but they can't seem to help themselves: it's as though Society Makes Them Do It. We do not completely understand why this came to be the case, and the topic probably merits its own volume (and one authored by somebody else), but we have tried to write in a straightforward manner. To the extent that we have failed, we have failed on our own and not because we have tried to sound like a sociologist. We have tried to use the clear language of everyday life even though we're speaking about something one does not normally discuss in everyday life. We have used contractions and changed agreement of number when it has suited the moment and done anything else we felt might better communicate the message.

- Finally, the thinking which drives the book is not derived from any one coherent body of theory, and—more to the point—the book is not directed at the elaboration of such a larger singular body of theory. Our approach is syncretic. Our intent is to apply the work of various sociological thinkers to the problem of explaining what makes people think as they do and not to advance the state of, for example, Symbolic Interactionism or Dialectical Materialism. By way of metaphor, you might say that we are trying to extract a technology from these older bodies of thought ... much as a radio engineer tries to extract wireless communications technology from radio physics. Technology can and frequently does impact back upon its theoretical milieu, but it need not. A legitimate scholar has a responsibility to his or her community to undertake work specifically because it contributes to a body of theory in his or her field and to evaluate the work of others in the light of its impact upon this body of theory. This is an enormously worthy business, but it is not specifically our business.

The book gathers itself, substantively and logically, into three sections:

- Chapters I through V create a theoretical framework for the analysis of the subject. Creation of this framework involves more than a theory of ideology; it includes a theory of society and culture. Those who really have no stomach for reading unvarnished sociology might be tempted to skip the first section. For the constitutionally robust, though, an understanding of this first section will contribute enormously to the understanding of what comes next. The two following sections make assertions based upon the theoretical structure constructed in the first section.

- Chapters VI through X comprise an analysis of contemporary American ideologies. This section introduces the notion that the two most important sectors of twenty-first century American society are the "yeomanry" and the "cognoscenti," societal sectors with their own identifiable positions in our society and ideologies which correspond to and reflect those different positions.

- Chapters XI and XII treat two important consequences of the analysis. One we call the Political Problem: How Do We Live Together? The other we call the Epistemological Problem: How Do We Know What To Believe?

By way of summary: we have proposed a theoretical framework which explains people's ideology—very broadly speaking, their political and social beliefs—in terms of their position in social groups and institutions, and which explains the structure of such social groups and institutions as being consequences of the technological and economic basis of the society. We then—in Section Two—apply this framework to contemporary American society and document the existence of two separate and conflicting sectors:

- What we have called the "yeomanry:" those people defined by their association with primary and secondary industry and the consequences of this for their relationship to formal organization (think "bureaucracy"), viz., that they exist on the *outsides* of formal organizations,

- What we have called the "cognoscenti:" those people defined by their association with tertiary industry and the consequences of this for their relationship to formal organization, viz., that they exist on the *insides* of formal organizations.

Now, why—it might fairly be asked—spend so much time creating a theoretical foundation for an accounting of our current political circumstance? A theoretical foundation turns what would otherwise be a mere descriptive narrative into an analysis, an analysis which makes possible prediction but which, even more, makes possible a comprehensive *understanding* of the constellation of the observed facts. We hope to provide the reader with not simply a set of factual assertions but with a theoretical framework to connect these facts and others of which the reader may be aware. Moreover, theory has its own aesthetic: ordered facts are more beautiful—indeed, much more beautiful—than disordered facts. There are different ways of ordering facts: one may order them into a taxonomy or order them into a theory. And a taxonomy and a theory are different things. A taxonomy groups similar facts into separate categories or bins: facts A1, A2 and A3 into one bin and facts B1, B2 and B3 into another. A theory, by contrast, may begin with a taxonomy but will then impose a *causal structure* upon these organized facts such that the theory argues that, for example, A1 *causes* B1, A2 *causes* B2, and so on.

And Section Three, finally, offers policy suggestions for defusing the dangers posed by the yeomanry/cognoscenti divide and offers suggestions about how to think about one's own thinking.

II. WHY DO PEOPLE BELIEVE AS THEY DO?

THIS IS, OF COURSE, A monumental question. We have beliefs, and we're aware that we have such beliefs, and that other people have beliefs as well, beliefs with which we might agree or disagree. The reader will, for instance, believe that he or she has just read this sentence. Moreover, if a friend were to be sitting beside you while you read and were to audibly read the sentence to you, you would agree that the friend has read—and believes that he or she has just read—the same sentence. The portion of mental functioning concerned with knowing and believing is called "cognition," and cognitive activity (as distinct from other kinds of mental activity, like emotions) represents a large part of what a mind consciously does during a typical day.

Much of cognition is based upon clear observation of relatively simple phenomena:

- There are two birds on the telephone wire.

- My friend is sitting in that chair.

- I have $52 in bills in my wallet and $1.23 in change in my pocket.

Such phenomena, which can be empirically verified (that is, you can observe or measure them), we call "facts."

Cognitive activity—the "knowing and believing" part of thinking—can be viewed as a continuum of verifiability with such plain facts on the left end and completely unverifiable propositions at the right end. Such unverifiable propositions ("God is love;" "Life is a fountain.") are necessarily taken on the basis of faith. This absence of verifiability doesn't mean anything about their truth value; it only says that they are not subject to empirical verification: you can't make observations to "test" their truthfulness.

The kinds of beliefs chiefly concerning us here lie midway on this continuum. These beliefs we will call "ideology," and ideology has certain qualitative characteristics:

- Ideology consists of beliefs about people and their behavior rather than about natural or physical phenomena unrelated to human activities.

- Ideology involves beliefs both about how things in life *are* or *were* (which is at least potentially testable) *and* beliefs about how things *ought to be* (which is much more difficult–indeed, often impossible–to test).

- Particular ideologies are characteristic of particular social groups of people: economic groups, ethnic groups, regional groups, etc.

So, we are examining the middle region of this continuum:

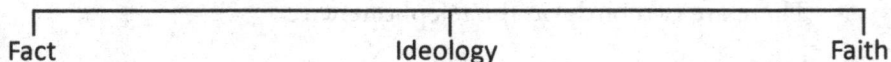

```
┌─────────────────────────┬─────────────────────────┐
Fact                   Ideology                    Faith
```

And the most interesting thing—the thing that we are going to try to explain—is why different *groups* of people have different ideologies …

different beliefs about things that are, at least to some extent, testable and verifiable. This approach—which we will call "ideological analysis"—is really much more usefully applicable to ideologies than to phenomena close to either pole of the continuum. There are (at least outside of academia) not many disputes about the simplest facts; there isn't any real dispute about whether you have $52 in your wallet if that's what you count when you look. An academic might argue that the $52 isn't worth what it used to be, or that it doesn't represent any real transcendent value at all. Those, of course, were not the questions: you have $52 in your wallet. The ideological part of the statement that "I see the glass as being half full; you see it as being half empty" is the implication that the former view is better than the latter; at the end of the day, you've got a half a glass of water (or some more convivial liquid).

By the same token, matters of pure faith—while they certainly characterize and distinguish identifiable groups of people—so clearly derive from how these people have been taught and trained and supported in these beliefs by their respective communities that this offers an adequate explanation of why they believe what they believe. To know that Roman Catholics are more prone to subscribe to Catholic beliefs like transubstantiation than are, say, Orthodox Jews is true but not at all interesting. Having said this, however, we shall eventually revisit faith; for the understanding of why faith can come to supplant observation and reason in the middle of the continuum above—in the province of ideology—will be critical to our understanding of why people believe as they do.

The distinctive characteristics of ideology outlined above will be found, as we proceed through our topic, to be true only in general. For instance, we have said that ideology pertains to ideas about human—rather than natural and physical—phenomena; however, one will frequently hear assertions that, for instance, the theory of evolution (as an explanation for phylogenetic differentiation) is reflective of a "capitalistic world view" (on account of its incorporation of concepts such as "competition," "survival of the fittest," etc.). In this case, the person is making an ideological assertion about the ideological character of biological theorizing in Western scientific thought. Another interesting example of an impact of ideology on "hard science" is Lysenkoism, an alternative to Mendelian genetics propounded in the old Soviet Union in the late 1920s and early 1930s by a Ukrainian agronomist named T. D. Lysenko. Lysenkoism enjoyed great currency during the Stalinist period because Communist ideologists saw some incompatibilities between Mendelian genetics and Marxist revolutionary theory. The Mendelian model, of course, ultimately prevailed (itself to be supplanted by the modern revolution in molecular biology), but the instance illustrates the power which an ideology can assume when backed by the might of the state.

A. ORGANIZING PRINCIPLES OF THE ARGUMENT

At one level it would seem simple, clean, and intellectually useful to take the following approach to the problem of why people believe as they do: people are either *correct* or more or less *incorrect* in their thinking, and to the extent that they are incorrect they are so because they are ill-informed, dishonest, biased, mentally incompetent, etc., or some combination of these and other distorting factors. Now, that may be true, but that is not how we are going to think about the problem. An approach may be intellectually coherent but not useful, and that is the situation here. First, what is "correct," especially in matters of political relevance, is not always clear. Moreover, finding out the "correct" view is not (at least in a simple sense) our job: we are supposed to be developing an explanation for *why* different groups of people believe different things to be correct, not whether those views *are* actually correct. Furthermore (and this is more important), to center the question of why somebody believes a certain thing on that individual believer (and how well-informed, honest, lucid, etc. the believer is) would deflect us from examining the social and historical structures and forces that cause identifiable groups to believe and think as they do. For us, the unit of analysis is only sometimes the individual; instead, we will mostly examine economic and techno-logical forces and events which subsequently govern the structure of social organization ... like the formation of social classes, occupational groups, the organization of the family and other social institutions. The individual, who lives his or her life in some particular social organization, will, ultimately, get a particular set of inputs, interests, etc., based on these life experiences which will influence what he or she believes, and these inputs will be structured according to what part of social organiza-tion (e.g., as a housewife or a corporate accountant) they have lived in. We are hoping to explain why groups or categories of individuals think as they do, and, consequently, we must understand how these groups or categories come into existence and how they operate. We realize that all this might seem either unnecessary or trivial; it is not, and we hope that, by the end of the book, the distinction will be clear to the reader. Heaven knows, we don't want to drag our gentle reader into the old fight between psychologists and sociologists about "reductionism" (and, to be sure, the reader doesn't wish to be so dragged), even though this battle—this primeval slime-storm—is exactly the issue. For purposes of this analysis, we simply must use groups and categories of people as units of analysis. And it is only because we will use groups—rather than individuals—as our units of analysis that we can offer pronouncements about phenomena on a societal level. Yes, societies consist (in part) of individuals, but these individuals are organized and can be categorized into groups, and this level of analysis grants us the capacity to make pronouncements at the societal level.

So, we will organize the argument around groups and categories of people rather than around individual persons—and their thought processes—themselves. Our approach has two consequences, both of them positive.

First of all (and this topic we will revisit), it steers us away from looking, in the first instance, to find the "principles," or "values," or "ideals" that people presumably hold and which allegedly determine what else they believe. There are several problems in trying to explain one group of widely held ideas by another: the "principle" and the "belief" will typically sound pretty similar, so that such explanations end up sounding suspiciously tautological—that is, they explain something with reference to itself—and you end up with propositions that have the form of "A is true because A is true." You might imagine, by way of a *Gedankexperiment*, doing research on the determination of democratic *beliefs* by democratic *principles*. If you collect data from individuals, you will have to ask these subjects questions about what they believe regarding things democratic: presumably, the questions about "beliefs" will be more specific, while the questions about "principles" will be more general; you might even create "latent factors" based on a formal statistical treatment of the answers to several questions clustered together. At the end of the day, though, the separation of "belief" and "principle"—of putative effect and cause— will have to completed conceptually by the analyst of the data, and one set of answers will be labeled "belief" and some other set of answers "principle." We will, happily, not face this problem.

Second, and even more significantly, choosing to organize our argument around groups, categories, economic forces, historical events, and other phenomena *exterior* to the individual allows us to draw from a deep and salubrious theoretical well. This tradition is called the "sociology of knowledge," or *Wissensociologie*, and it counts among its contributors some of the best minds in Western social thought from the nineteenth and twentieth centuries. Having this resource means that we don't have to start into this enterprise without some useful tools. The people who have put most of the tools into our kit are Karl Marx, Karl Mannheim, David Riesman, and Peter Berger. This book, whatever else it is, represents a twenty-first century application of the ideas of these gentlemen as well as some others. It's not that there is nothing new that is good; it's just that some very useful thinking was done over the past century and a half, and we shall utilize it.

B. THE SOCIOLOGY OF KNOWLEDGE

The very name "sociology of knowledge" is, though not really a misnomer, a bit confusing. Most of the original theoretical work in the field was done in German—most notably with contributions by Karl Marx and Karl Mannheim—and the name "sociology of knowledge" is a literal translation of the German noun *"Wissensociologie,"* a noun which is formed (as is frequently done in the German linguistic tradition), by combining two existing nouns. Though *"Wissen"* can be translated into English to mean "knowledge," it can also be understood to mean "belief" or "understanding," and the latter would, for our purposes, have been a better rendering: better because so much of what the sociology of knowledge deals with material of debatable truth or "knowledge" value.

There are several theoretical traditions in the sociology of knowledge, and it is not our business to discuss nor even to identify them. Readers who want to delve more deeply into these traditions are encouraged to work from the materials cited in the book and other sources.

The core notion—the belief which binds all of these traditions together into what can be called a sociology of knowledge—is that individuals' ideas can be predicted and/or explained by their social positions. Thus, by knowing an individual's social group memberships, you should be able to understand something about what he or she believes. We are using the term "group" to mean any identifiable category or collection of people; some sociologists restrict the term to collections of people actually interacting with one another. Now, the sorts of social groups which have been identified as influencing thought have included social classes, occupational groups, industries, the two genders, and many others. At this level, the reader can likely identify, in his or her own experience, differences in thinking or attitude that are associated with different groups. Certainly, such perceived differences between groups are the basis for a good deal of humor: all those jokes based on the differences between engineers versus non-engineers, or men versus women, or marketers versus accountants and how they look at the world take advantage of these alleged cognitive differences. Political campaigning relies on different pitches being made (often by the same candidate) to different constituencies: health care reform is pitched to labor union constituencies, tax reform to corporate executives, social security reform to members of the American Association of Retired Persons.

In general, the large and obvious differences between national cultures and large regional cultures are not subject to analysis by the sociology of knowledge, the consensus being that once something gets into a culture, the culture tends to maintain it by the normal mechanisms of cultural transmission. Thus, the fact that the citizens of Japan characteristically speak Japanese and do other things in a Japanese way—and that the citizens of Iceland do not—though true, is not very interesting. On the other hand, a practitioner of the sociology of knowledge might try to characterize the culture of island nations (like Japan, Iceland, the United Kingdom, etc.) and distinguish broad common traits among them by contrasting them with the cultural traits of continental nations and their cultures by using the very insularity of living on an island to account for these (if there are any) commonalties.

We, however, will select economic and technological factors to account for the ideological differences we observe in American culture today and to account for the changes we have seen in American culture over time. We make this choice because economic and technological factors appear to be the most effective agents (and the book's entire thesis is an argument that this is so) for explaining what we see. Moreover, the founders of the sociology of knowledge tradition, chiefly Marx and Mannheim, substantially share this view and, thus, provide us with the elements of a theoretical framework to account for what we see. Let us now begin.

C. ECONOMY, SOCIETY AND IDEA

We are going to advance an approach to the problem which has three levels (and, thus, two strata of interaction among these three levels): the best way to understand both the nature of any society and the culture associated with this society is to start with the technology and economy that support—that make possible—that society. Explanations taking this form are called "materialistic" explanations and are contrasted with what are called "idealistic" explanations. Clearly, these two terms are being used differently from their use in conventional English: "materialistic" doesn't mean "craving money and material things;" it means "made of matter and energy;" "idealistic" doesn't mean "inspired by lofty motives;"

it means "made of ideas." If you explain the nature of American society and culture by citing the influence of a powerful industrial economy, you are making a materialistic explanation; if you make an explanation of American society and culture by citing the influence of democratic values, you are making an idealistic explanation. We are doing the former.

Economic and technological factors are (taken together) only one of the categories of "material" or "real" factors that have been employed to explain thought or character. Others have included natural resources, climate, race, and population size. All of these have the character of being somehow outside of the realm of human thought but capable of influencing or determining thought. The specific traditions from which we are working, however, accord primary importance to economic and technological factors.

"Economy" and "technology" are lumped together here for convenience, but they are, obviously, very different phenomena. By "economy" we mean the actual productive processes by which a society creates or obtains the scarce goods and services necessary to sustain its population and support its activities. "Technology," on the other hand, consists of the knowledge available in the society's culture about how the world may be manipulated in a desired way. The economies of a hunting and gathering society, an agricultural society, a manufacturing-based industrial society, and an information-based post-industrial society such as the United States is coming to be, are clearly very different, and the technological differences characterizing them and enabling their economies are, just as clearly, an important dimension of what distinguishes them. What is more, the importance of technology as a driver of historical social change goes to the issue of the role of the individual human mind in the scheme of things as we have been describing it. A misreading of the materialistic view is that ideas have no impact back on the society or its economy; this is clearly incorrect: fire-making, the moldboard plow, the steam engine, packet switching, artificial intelligence (AI) ... all started out as ideas in somebody's mind, and they have all clearly had colossal impacts on economic production and the human condition. Technological ideas impact material reality. To advance a materialistic explanation of ideologies is simply to choose, in an interactive process, that point which will best serve the job at hand. Our job is to account for ideological differences in American society, and the most useful organizing principle is to choose that set of factors most clearly proximate to and causal of the phenomena to be explained. For us, that set is the economy and the social groupings growing out of the prevailing economic order; clearly the economy and society are influenced in a profound way by the implementation of the technological ideas of individual humans.

We have discussed culture (the realm of shared ideas), social organization (the realm of social groups, organizations and institutions), and the economy (the realm of production based on technology, labor, capital, and resources). It is now time to provide a graphic to describe how these broad categories fit together.

Figure 1, on the next page, illustrates, in a block-diagrammatic way, how this all works.

Now, if this is beginning to sound distressingly like Sociology 101, we can only ask that the reader indulge us a bit longer. We will go through Figure 1 step by step so that the reader can acquire a general sense for the argument. Then we will proceed to the important points that, in a rapidly changing industrial society, it will invariably be the case that there are multiple and conflicting structures of this sort—*each based upon a particular mode of production*—and that it is this multiplicity that gives rise to ideological conflict. Then, happily, we will proceed to real cases.

FIGURE 1. ECONOMY, SOCIETY AND CULTURE

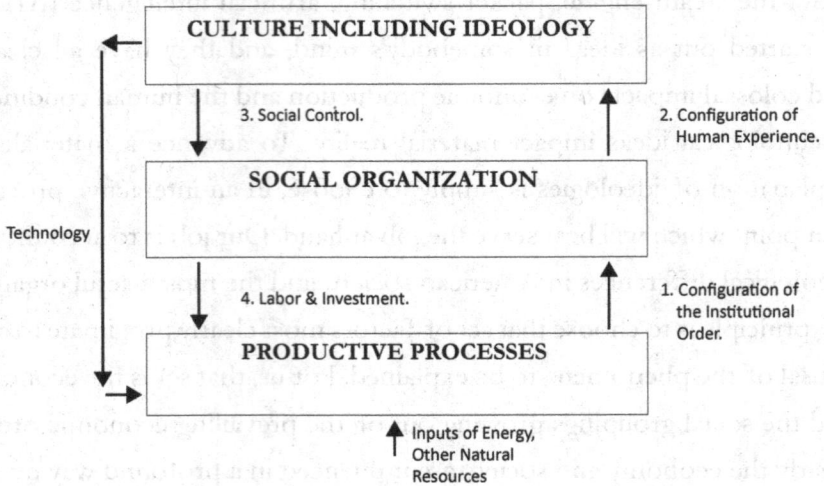

CULTURE INCLUDING IDEOLOGY

3. Social Control.

2. Configuration of Human Experience.

SOCIAL ORGANIZATION

Technology

4. Labor & Investment.

1. Configuration of the Institutional Order.

PRODUCTIVE PROCESSES

Inputs of Energy, Other Natural Resources

Sociology 101 cracks aside, Figure 1 is the most important summarizing object in this first section of the book. It is a graphic representation of the theory of society and culture which underlies and animates this book and the arguments herein.

The reader has not been presented with just a model of a sociology of ideology. *This is a model of a sociology.* Moreover, this is a model of a sociology as a life science: not a sociology as a history of ideas, nor as a "history of oppression," nor as the "arc of history bending toward" some aspirational state or another. This is a theory of how matter in motion evolved into a social form in association with the species *Homo sapiens*. This is a theory—and an associated model—not merely of ideology but of human sociality itself.

1. Economy and Society: The Configuration of the Institutional Order.

We are suggesting, first of all, that the nature of production determines the nature of social order, that a particular way of producing will configure a society's institutions in a way that reflects this way of producing. Some social forms are simply not possible given a particular economic dispensation, and—since the impossible never happens—there is an empirical relationship between the industrial base of a society and its social structure. Some of this is obvious: all pre-industrial societies, for example, have characteristics distinguishing them from all industrial societies, and these differences arise from differing modes of production. Pre-industrial societies are based upon modes of production which are:

- Limited, in the sense that machines are simple, not much energy is captured from the environment, populations are locally small,

- Slow to change,

- Not reliant on specialized technology nor the specialized labor skills needed to operate such technology.

By contrast, industrialized societies have powerful technologies which take a lot from the environment (and dump a lot of waste back into that environment), support lots of people on small amounts of land, change rapidly and require specialized technologies and their practitioners. How many of these occupational roles exist and what the roles consist of in terms of expected behavior are determined by industrial technologies.

These differences between the technological/industrial bases of pre-industrial and industrial societies give rise to certain differences in their social orders. For instance, the extended family structure (multiple generations and more distant relatives living together) so characteristic of most pre-industrial societies, generally disappears with industrialization. This is due largely the much higher rates of social and geographic mobility in industrial societies. Except among groups like the Amish or Hutterites in the USA—which actively avoid contact with the wider society and maintain an agrarian economy—the once-ubiquitous extended family form has essentially disappeared from the American social scene to be replaced by the nuclear family (parents and minor children living together). In pre-industrial societies, there is very little occupational specialization: in the simplest societies, age and gender are the only bases of specialization: men do one kind of work; women do another; old folks pontificate; and kids just play around. This lack of occupational specialization contrasts markedly with what we experience in the modern West where there are thousands of occupational specializations, and things change very rapidly such that entire occupations (e.g., DIBOL programmer) may arise and disappear in the space of an individual's working lifetime.

We will return to these issues later and in greater detail. Our purpose here is to illustrate the relationship between economy and society.

2. Society and Culture: The Configuration of Human Experience.

Most of the waking lives of individual human beings are lived in a social context: that is, not only do we live and interact with people, but we also act within a framework of social roles typical to our society, or, at least, to our part of it. So, a mother who is also a professional teacher doesn't interact with her own child in the same way she would with one of her students of the same age: she changes roles when she puts down her ruler and puts on her apron. A worker responds differently to a boss than to a coworker. Our social roles are provided by our society, and we learn to conduct ourselves within them: worker, mother, Deputy Assistant Secretary of Defense for Intelligence, all the rest. We humans are, of course, aware creatures and heavily influenced by our experience; most of this experience is, as we have noted, conducted within the social roles which we are given … and we've already seen where the roles come from.

Most of the information which presents itself to us comes by virtue of our incumbency in the set of roles which we assume. Therefore, and to the extent that we actually learn and internalize this information, our learned ideas and awareness are formed by our social experience. And this social experience doesn't just serve to structure what we *learn*; it also influences such new ideas as we might *create* or generate (a tax attorney probably isn't, for example, as likely to come up with a new way to mine coal as is a mining engineer), and it certainly influences our *receptivity* to ideas presented to us. To say it another way: our social positions impact the likelihood that we will *create, transmit, or be receptive to* certain ideas. Our roles, for instance, provide us with material interests, and people commonly support ideas that promote their material interests. Ranchers who graze cattle on public lands support the idea of maintaining below-market grazing fees; operators of export firms support the idea of Most Favored Nation trading status for China; African American people support the idea of racial preferences for African Americans, on and on.

Too much can be made of material interest as a determinant of ideological position, however; Heaven knows, people support ideas detrimental to their own interests; indeed, whole *groups* of people support ideas—in the form of ideologies successfully mediated to them by other groups—which are contrary to their own interests. *There's a lot more going on here than just material interest.*

For the sake of getting through this part of the argument, let us out-
line, in summary fashion, some candidate explanations (none of them
mutually exclusive) of how people in certain social positions might be
attracted to certain ideologies:

- People are often attracted to ideas that serve either their personal
  or their membership groups' interests.

- People also support ideas which they are paid or otherwise
  induced to support by groups of which they are not members.
  In these cases, the client group has extended its interest to its
  representative by inducing that person to support its position.

- People can be induced to support ideas because these ideas are
  mediated to them by some high-status group or individual. These
  are matters of fashion, and ideologies can be more or less fashionable, depending upon the groups associated with that ideology
  and the quality of the ideas' mediation.

- People tend to support ideas which are compatible with, or which
  make sense of their own situations, even when these ideas might
  not be in their interests. For instance, most small businesspeople
  are antagonistic toward federal government deficit spending;
  this includes businesspeople who might even benefit from such
  spending. One explanation is that businesspeople are simply
  uncomfortable with perennially expanding deficits because it's
  not a fiscal practice compatible with their own situations: their
  own bankers won't let them continue to accumulate deficits. What
  in the hell are they doing back there in Washington?

- People tend to believe what those around them believe. If people
  acquire an ideology, and all of those around them subscribe to

the same ideology, they are unlikely to question or challenge that ideology. Indeed, in situations of seamless ideological homogeneity, they may not be able to *conceive* of a way of looking at things which disagrees with what their group supports (Such situations of unrippled ideological homogeneity are rare but exist in the most remote hunting and gathering societies and among groups of post-modern literary critics).

• People believe what they are taught to believe, which is the normal way culture is transmitted from one generation to another.

By one mechanism or another, people in different groups take on positions which reflect their membership in these groups. We see this in everyday life, and we expect that people in different social positions will have predictable cultural styles or points of view on ideological matters. We expect booming, grinning, back-slapping confidence in a marketing man; we expect that an academic in a Liberal Arts department will have Leftist points of view on any issue which has a Left side; we expect parochialism from small-scale farmers; we anticipate a sort of Rotarian Babbittry from small-town business people. So, there's nothing revolutionary in what you've just been told; you knew it all the time. One of the things that this book wants to provide you is a theoretical framework on which to hang what you've seen in life.

3. Social Control: The Impact of Ideas on the Social Order.

We have said that technological ideas impact human life, but so, too, do ideas about the social order and proper behavior therein. It is easy to see, for instance, that ideas like "work hard, and you will be rewarded" that reflect, however imperfectly, life in a capitalist industrial society, might act back on that society: to the extent that these ideas are celebrated currently and transmitted to the next generation, people will work hard at their jobs and support the institutional order. The same can be said for a cultural idea—an item of ideology—that "good people don't steal." This norm has been incorporated into the law. When most people obey the laws of the land—as they currently do in the United States—the law is mediated into the culture as a powerful ideology. This, in turn, allows it to be an effective means of social control, *even when most people are never subject to the sorts of legal penalties which attend disobedience to the law.*

In fact, the sort of social control exerted by that part of the culture which we call "norms"—socially accepted rules for behavior—is only one kind of social control. We shall call it "internal social control" because it relies on individuals internalizing and accepting as legitimate these cultural rules. And, given that human behavior has to be controlled in a society (virtually by definition), it is far and away the most efficient kind of social control. The other sort of social control is (obviously) *external* social control. This social control is affected through explicit positive and negative inducements: if you behave well, you get a reward; if you behave poorly, you get punished. If society had to rely only upon external social control, society would be impossible: no society could afford the numbers of law enforcers and supervisors necessary to achieve adequate and proper behavior; it would require more cops and managers than citizens ... and who would manage and police the police and the managers? Happily, people aren't like that. In all surviving societies, most people refrain from, for example, shoplifting not just because they're afraid of going to jail; rather, they refrain from shoplifting because they understand that good people don't do that sort of thing ... and that's what they teach their kids. In fact, the kind of societies in which our humankind evolved relied almost exclusively on internal social control: the occupational specializations of police officer and paymaster are relatively recent innovations. Small societies are, in that sense, more efficient to operate because the sort of control necessary for proper societal operation comes out of the traditional culture, and this culture is a powerful force because these societies are very homogeneous both in space and in time: that is, there are not very many different kinds of people in the society, and the society doesn't change much over time.

Now, we have called this particular moment in the larger process "social control," which sounds like a pretty conservative label for a process which could theoretically be used to change the society's way of doing things as well as preserving existing arrangements. After all, internal social control operates at the level of norms—rules which say, for example, "work hard and be rewarded"—and it is, presumably, possible for powerful operators to change the publicly-articulated rule to: "lie around, scratch your privates, and be rewarded" and thus destabilize the social order. Certainly, elements within the society advocate for social change, who have, indeed, made it central to their own ideology. If we are to be intellectually consistent, we must account for the existence of these elements themselves and do so in a manner consistent with the model we are developing (remember, this is all supposed to well up from the mode of production to the nature of social organization to the culture). For this accounting, we will need to introduce another notion—the notion of multiple structures existing in the same society—and this we will do in Chapter V below.

4. Labor and Investment: Factors of Production.

The reader should understand that the distinction which we have drawn between an occupational role and its status as a factor of production is a conceptual distinction; that is, these two entities exist in the same place and at the same time, but they are, for purposes of this framework, different things. They are different, but a worker operating in some recognized occupational role (e.g., Python programmer) doesn't have to go anyplace or do anything special to be *both* an incumbent of a social role *and* a factor of production ("labor") in the production process. Any economic order requires that certain inputs be obtained: these are the famous "land, labor, and capital." In fact, these (particularly "land") are a bit metaphorical, and the economy needs natural resource inputs, including energy, adequately trained labor, the surplus wealth that is called "capital," as well as the shared knowledge about how you produce goods and services that we call "technology."

This entire analysis assumes, of course, that energy must be brought into the social system and that the social system is an energy-capturing entity. This description makes the social system sound like something living—particularly because it also reproduces itself and endures over time; in fact, there existed, in the nineteenth century, a sociological tradition which is recalled as "organicism," which argued that societies are in some very real sense "alive." Organicism—including its more extreme variant "bio-organicism"—doesn't enjoy much currency in sociological circles today, but there isn't any doubt that societies use energy to function and that features of social organization bring energy into the society. This reality is, perhaps, most explicitly recognized in the theoretical tradition which emerged in the late twentieth century called "sociobiology" which is associated with the name of the late Edwin O. Wilson[1] and which emerged from the departments of biology rather than departments of sociology. In this view, society is regarded as a sort of external and collective organ cropping up at various points on the phylogenetic scale: ants, bees, geese, herring, mole rats, cattle, wolves, humans and many others.

Now, to digress a bit to extend this last point, let us note that we do subscribe to the view that sociology is a life science (prior and in addition to its being a social science) in the pivotally important sense that there are only sociologies of living things. There is a sociology of human societies; there is a sociology of animals: sociobiology as described above; there is, many would argue, a sociology of plants.[2] Indeed, recent botanical research has revealed an instance of "eusociality" (intensive sociality, in this case, specialized roles in support of reproduction) in the epiphytic fern *Platycerium bifurcatum*[3].

There is no sociology of stones.

Societies may be thought of as being the external and collective organs of the social species with which they are associated. And—as living things which exist in a material environment—human societies evolve but evolve in a particular way. Evolution involves the adaptation of a species of living thing to its environment. *And the unique thing about the evolution of human societies is that—whereas other living things use anatomical and physiological features (including, of course, those features which permit sociality) to mediate between themselves and their environments—human societies use technology*

1. Edwin O. Wilson, *Sociobiology: The New Synthesis* (Cambridge, Massachusetts: Harvard University Press, 1975).

2. Peter Wohlbein, *The Hidden Life of Trees* (Vancouver: Greystone Books, 2016).

3. Kevin C. Burns, *On the selective advantage of coloniality in staghorn ferns (Platycerium bifurcatum, Polypodiaceae)* (National Library of Medicine, Plant Signaling and Behavior, August 2, 2021) https://www.ncbi.nlm.nih.gov/pmc/articles/PMC8525959/

to mediate between themselves and their environments. Further, in human societies, the salience of technological change comes, over time, to largely supplant the salience of biological evolution in determining the nature of human social life and, thus, human experience.

Life—all life—is information, information which has the capacity to re-write itself in order to reproduce and endure in time, and this information is coded as DNA or RNA. But evolution requires a further step: some source of variation in this process of re-writing to permit adaptation to new or changing environments *via* natural selection. The principal sources of this variation are genetic mutation and sexual reproduction which permits the mixing of genomes. This view of life as information interestingly implies that the organism is the genome's way of reproducing the genome rather than the other way around. Evolution—the process of adaptive change to suit the organism to new and changing environments—takes enormous amounts of time. In fact, the theory of biological evolution required the idea of geologic time to be developed and documented by geologists in order to proceed to its present state of maturity, and fully adequate evidence for the reality of geologic time did not happen (according to some sources) until 1911.[4] This huge time requirement of biological evolution exists because such evolution is always "evolution from" a state of being, never "evolution to" a state of being. In philosophical terms, biological evolution is "non-teleological;" that is, there is nothing in the genome which "steers" it toward some future state.

Technology (as a form of culture) is different. Technological innovation—reliant as it is on human creativity—is almost always anticipatory:

---

4. Science Daily, *How The Discovery Of Geologic Time Changed Our View Of The World* (University of Bristol, 2007, accessed 20221) https://www.sciencedaily.com/releases/2007/09/07091308 1021.htm

a new state of being is almost always envisioned in technological innovation. The inventor envisions his or her invention prior to inventing it. To be a bit glib about it: biological evolution links humans to the past; technological innovation links humans to the future.

This anticipatory nature of technological innovation enormously accelerates the rate of change of human societies relative to other societies—bovine, avian, insect, etc.—which rely only upon biological evolution. Human societies evolve, but evolve within the context of human technological innovation, and this makes human societies unique among societies of living things. Thus, a science of human sociality is going to be different from a science of general (animal, plant, etc.) sociality in an important way: the "cultural level" in Figure 1—and particularly the technological component of culture—is going to be absent or minimal in the case of a non-human society. Yes, there are indications of culture, and even technology, in some animals, but these are miniscule in contrast to even the simplest human societies. Non-human organisms do, indeed, share information between and among individual organisms but not *via* the medium of culture.

Technology isn't a feature of ant or bovine society and economic production, but it certainly is a feature of human society and economic production. In fact, technology is the most interesting feature of human economic production not just because it distinguishes us from the rest of the biosphere but because the efficacy of technology is so different among societies and because, in the case of late-phase industrial societies, it changes at a stunning rate.

The "Hand-held Stone Ax" tradition persisted in the Western Desert of Australia for fifty thousand years, a staggering case of technological conservatism. This means that this core technology—the use of an unhafted stone ax to do anything that you can do with an unhafted stone ax—persisted for at least a sixth of the three hundred-thousand year period of *Homo sapiens'* existence on the planet,[5] and for the entire pre-contact period of existence of the species in Australia. This sort of technological conservatism will, if you follow our model, lead to extreme social conservatism, to extreme cultural conservatism, and so on down through the system. And this is, in fact, the case.

Societies such as the aboriginal society in the Western Desert were dominated in their every element by negative feedback loops: every aspect of the economy, the society and the culture operate to conserve the existing structure. The economy never produces very much, so the population and the number of different kinds of people in the society never grows very large nor elaborate. The culture doesn't change much, so the social control works very well, and the technology, capital, and labor inputs into economy are never very large, so the system just persists and persists … in this case for fifty thousand years, essentially until Europeans came in and kicked out the jams. The systems theory notion of a negative feedback loop—which is a general conception for a stabilizing control mechanism (e.g., a household thermostat which turns the furnace on as the room cools down and turns it off as the room heats up)—is an awfully compelling model for the entire operation these sorts of societies.

What it takes to destabilize these sorts of smoothly functioning systems is a big increase or decrease *at any point in the system*: if, for example, somehow a modern social institutional order could be created and supported out of nothingness, then the process of change would be initiated. But creating (as opposed to importing, which happened in the case of post-contact Australia) something material out of nothingness is an impossibility. The unique feature of technology is that it is made up

5. David Reich, *Who We Are and How We Got Here* (New York: Pantheon Books, 2018), p. 2.

out of ideas in the creative imaginations of certain human beings. Now, it's clear that some kinds of societies—the big, industrial kind—are much better at generating new technologies than are others. It's clear, too, that it takes material surpluses to conduct the sort of research and development needed to generate these technologies and that it costs money—sometimes colossal amounts of money—to implement new technologies into industrial production. But the fact remains that technology is a product of the human mind, and, thus, is the easiest point in the entire social system for change to begin. And, once begun, this change transforms what had been negative feedback loops into positive feedback loops: the more technologically induced economic and social change occurs, the more social and cultural change is spawned. Positive feedback loops are used to model such growth mechanisms: the bigger a seedling gets, the larger its root area, and the faster it can grow; the larger a culture of mold on a petri dish grows, the more organisms there are to reproduce, and the faster it grows.

So, societies vary in their technologies from one to another and, within societies, over time. Technology ends up being a critical element in understanding what makes societies operate as they do and, by our model, in understanding what sorts of ideas people in these societies will create and support.

What is more, technology gives us a very powerful explanation for social change on the most general level. Technology is clearly a mental production of human beings, and it is this kind of mental production—the kind that makes it possible to manipulate the natural and physical worlds—that has a determinative impact upon economic production, that is, upon how much a human society can take out of the natural and physical worlds and what it can do with these resources. We've already considered the way economy impacts social organization. Thus, any accounting for social and cultural change over time—that is, for the process of history—which neglects technology is very flawed, indeed. It is the engineer who is the apostle of change.

Now, one might ask—since we're talking about "social change"—how about ideological ideas themselves as candidates for creating social change? We're talking about "revolutionary" ideological ideas—ideas intended to destabilize the existing social order. We are persuaded that "revolutionary" ideas are more usefully regarded as a cultural expression of social change than as a precipitator of social change: as more of an "effect" than a "cause." In Chapter VII we shall trace such "revolutionary" ideology to the emergence of specific social groups that appear in consequence of the emergence of new modes of production made possible by new technologies.

III. TECHNOLOGY AND IDEOLOGICAL DIFFERENTIATION

IN THE PRECEDING CHAPTER, we have outlined a framework relating economy to social organization and social organization to ideology and to culture more generally. We have also argued for a special role for technology in accounting for the differences between different sorts of societies and in accounting for differences in the same society over time (that is, social change). This analysis has owed—though we have not said so yet—a great deal to the seminal ideas of Karl Marx in his thinking about the relationship between economic production (which he is generally translated to call the "mode of production") and social order, *and* between social order (referred to in some English translations as the "relations of production") and ideology. One might have occasion to read a Marxian scholar discussing the relationship between "substructure" ("*Unterbau*") or relations of production and "superstructure" ("*Ueberbau*") or ideology, these terms referring to Marx's view of the relationship between the relations of production and ideology. For Marx, the single overwhelmingly important aspect of any set of relations of production is the contemporaneously existing class order. By applying a theory of change which he inherited from the German philosopher

Hegel (this is the famous "dialectic") to this conception of the social world as being dominated by the class system, Marx generates the theory of social revolution for which he is most principally famous:

> "The history of all hitherto existing society is the history of class struggles. Freeman and slave, patrician and plebeian, lord and serf, guild-master and journeyman, in a word: oppressor and oppressed ... ."[6].

The revolutionary theory of Marx is not a part of our own analysis, and this is not the place to delve into that part of Marx more deeply than the bare skimming we have just provided. Some may find the involvement of Marx in any sort of analysis very off-putting, but this is a part of the history of the field in which we are operating. Rest assured, you can read the following without being or becoming a social revolutionary or Social Justice Warrior (not that there's anything wrong with that; we just don't think that it's sociology's job.)[7].

It is from Marx that we take the fundamental ideas that there is a relationship between economy and society:

> ... a certain mode of production, or industrial stage, is always combined with a certain mode of co-operation, or social stage...[8]

and that there is a relationship between consciousness—or idea—and social organization:

> Consciousness is therefore from the very beginning a social product and remains so as long as men exist at all.[9]

---

6. Karl Marx, *The Communist Manifesto* (Toronto: Vanguard, nd), p. 26.

7. If you're still bothered about reading something originally thought up by a commie, I can't help you: don't read this; go read the funny papers.

8. Karl Marx, *The German Ideology*, (New York: International Publishers, 1947), p. 18.

9. *Ibid.*, p. 19.

The structure represented by Figure 1 and described in the foregoing chapter portrays a society and its associated economy and culture as if there were only one economic order—or, at least, a uniform economic order—associated with the society. This is the case with very simple, small, and slow-changing societies, but it is not the case with industrial societies. *In industrial societies there are multiple modes of economic production and, therefore, multiple social groupings and multiple cultural expressions of these groupings, i.e., ideology.*

The coarsest way one might categorize the economic activity which is going on in a society is to categorize this activity into "industrial sectors." The most broadly accepted of these taxonomies divides the economy of a modern society into three sectors:

- Primary industry—or "extractive" industry, such as farming, mining, petroleum extraction, hunting, fishing, timber harvest, or other economic activity which extracts resources directly from the physical environment,

- Secondary industry—or manufacturing industry, which involves the production of goods from highly processed resources, the production, for example, of the chair in which you are sitting,

- Tertiary industry—or service industry, which provides valuable things which neither have weight nor take up space such as, for example, medical care, the advice provided by an accountant, or the lessons of a teacher or any sort of consultation service.

One obvious point about this classification is that these industrial types have an historical sequence: primary industry appears first, and the simpler societies—hunting and gathering through agricultural societies—possess only this sector. Secondary industry appeared, at least in a world-changing way, with the Industrial Revolution, approximately two centuries ago in Europe. Tertiary industry is newer (again, as a dominant economic activity; shamans were very early representatives of the service sector, though they were generally amateurs). In the case of societies like the USA, all three industrial forms are represented, though they appear in this same sequence historically, and, consequently, the society may be described as being dominated chiefly by one or the other industrial forms at different times. The 1880 census of the United States revealed that 49 percent of the population was engaged in farm work,[10] so it might be said that this was the point when agriculture (and extractive industries generally)—and the social and cultural forms associated with primary industry—yielded to manufacturing, secondary industry, as the form of economic activity setting the tone for the United States. The transition to tertiary industry in the United States—particularly to that vaunted portion of tertiary industry called the "information economy"—took much less time, less than a century, and might be said to have begun in this country in about 1960.

The forces propelling the United States through these social changes were principally technological changes: the combination of rational agricultural production and growing technological sophistication in manufacturing made it possible for more people to leave the food-production sector and made it, simultaneously, economically attractive for them to move to town and take these new factory jobs. The transition to an economy dominated by the service sector was occasioned by the needs in the manufacturing sector for increasingly sophisticated technologies and their practitioners (certainly engineers, but one would have to also acknowledge a growing need for the specialized skills of accountants, program managers, and other highly educated professionals), and the

---

10. Wayne C. Rohrer and Louis H. Douglas, *The Agrarian Transition in America* (New York: Bobbs-Merrill, 1969), p. 108.

incorporation into civilian industry of a device which appeared at the end of World War II: the electronic computer.

Now, it is frequently noted that in the United States we are currently living in the time of the "information economy" or in a nation gradually becoming dominated by its "service economy," but, in fact, the other parts of the economic order remain: there are still extractive and manufacturing sectors, though the proportions of the labor force that they constitute—and their respective values added—have grown proportionally smaller over time. This multi-sectored character of modern societies is very important and distinguishes them from earlier societal forms. It's not just that societies like the US are "industrialized" or "post-industrialized." They are that, but, in addition, they retain these historically older economic forms and the social and cultural patterns associated with them. Agrarian societies, for instance, don't have much of a manufacturing or service sector, but a society such as American society retains its primary and secondary sectors, and it is difficult to see how they would ever disappear because they provide economic goods which do not and inherently cannot have a "service" equivalent.

So, in reconsidering the framework we assembled in the last chapter as it applies to societies like the United States, one is constrained to say that any one of these structures (that is, the "Club Sandwich" in Figure 1) is not even a very good one-time snapshot of the society and its economy and culture. At best, it would represent a "blend" of the several sectors of the economy and the consequences that come along with that blend.

Marx suggests something similar to what we have proposed relative to the role of technology in creating different industrial orders (which create different social orders, which then create differing ideologies). Listen to him in *The German Ideology*:

Division of labour only becomes truly such from the moment when a division of material and mental labour appears. From this moment onwards consciousness can really flatter itself that it is something other than consciousness of existing practice, that it is really conceiving something without conceiving something real; from now on consciousness is in a position to emancipate itself from the real world and to proceed to the formation of "pure" theory, theology, philosophy, ethics, etc. But even if this theory, theology, philosophy, ethics, etc. comes into contradiction with the existing relations, this can only occur as a result of the fact that existing social relations have come into contradiction with existing forces of production; this, moreover, can also occur in a particular national sphere of relations through the appearance of the contradiction, not within the national orbit, but between this national consciousness and the practice of other nations, i.e., between the national and the general consciousness of a nation.

Moreover, it is quite immaterial what consciousness starts to do on its own: out of all such muck we get only the one inference that these three moments, the forces of production, the state of society, and the consciousness, can and must come into contradiction with one another ... .[11]

Not bad for a Dead White Male with a bad haircut writing one and a half centuries ago! Marx is leading into a subsequent topic, viz., the issue of class struggle and his dialectical theory of history (as well as saying something rather disparaging about the emergence and character of the social category we call "intellectuals"), and he is talking about conflicts within each of these economic/social/cultural structures

---

11. *Marx, op. cit.*, pp. 20-21.

themselves—among and between structures at these three levels. In addition, he suggests something a bit like what we have been talking about in that conflicts ("contradictions") on the ideological level will reflect conflicts on the more material levels.

This conflict between cultural ideas and the social order—a conflict which occurs because economic, social and cultural changes occur in a time-sequenced way due to the causal relationships between them—is sometimes referred to by sociologists by the term "cultural lag." The idea is that culture "lags behind" the social and economic changes which produce such cultural change. To cite a current example: our laws governing the "tech sector"—and particularly social media—have lagged far, far behind the technologies which make possible these industries. Cultural lag need not involve laws. Consider the change in American norms regarding sexual behavior which followed—lagging behind—the technological innovation of the birth control pill. Currently, state and federal laws governing privacy and publication are inadequate to properly govern what is being called the "synthetic media" including "deepfake" audio/video creations. The same could be said for AI, the capabilities of which are clearly expanding far more rapidly than they can be governed.

IV. THE SOCIAL PSYCHOLOGY OF IDEOLOGY

A. THE FORMULATION OF IDEOLOGIES AND THE ACCEPTANCE OF IDEOLOGIES BY INDIVIDUALS

HOW IS IT THAT IDEOLOGICAL ideas are formulated and then transmitted to and accepted by others? Another way to phrase this question is to break it in two: "What are the factors impacting the likelihood that one party will create and transmit an idea?" and "What are the factors impacting people's receptivity to the idea?"

Marx had something to say about this:

> The ideas of the ruling class are in every epoch the ruling ideas: i.e., the class, which is the ruling material force of society, is at the same time its ruling intellectual force. The class which has the means of material production at its disposal, has control at the same time over the means of mental production, so that thereby, generally speaking, the ideas of those who lack the means of mental production are subject to it. The ruling ideas are nothing

more than the ideal expression of the dominant material relationships, the dominant material relationships grasped as ideas; hence of the relationships which make the one class the ruling one, therefore the ideas of its dominance. The individuals composing the ruling class possess among other things consciousness, and therefore think. In so far, therefore, as they rule as a class and determine the extent and compass of an epoch, it is self-evident that they do this in their whole range, hence among other things rule also as thinkers, as producers of ideas, and regulate the production and distribution of the ideas of their age: thus their ideas are the ruling ideas of the epoch.[12]

We are not going to quarrel with the central thesis being expressed here: the ruling ideas of any age tend to be the ideas of its dominant groups. That's different from what Marx meant by "ruling class." In fact, we will frequently refer to this idea in the following pages. However, we need something more precise and something that provides for specific connections between forms of social organization and individual minds (which participate in a shared culture). Let us say, first of all, that we are searching for two sorts of factors:

- Those which increase the likelihood that somebody will actually *create and transmit* an idea,

- Those which increase the likelihood that somebody will *accept and retain* an idea.

Regarding both sets of factors, we will rely on a tradition within the sociology of knowledge which is most associated with the name of Peter Berger.[13]

---

12. *Ibid.*, p. 39.

13. See particularly Peter Berger and Thomas Luckmann, *The Social Construction of Reality* (Garden City: Doubleday Anchor, 1967).

Berger and his colleagues rely very heavily on the earlier social psychology of Alfred Schutz that emphasizes the prominence of *the experience of everyday life* in the formation of ideas.[14] The thrust of what we are doing in this book originates from the notion that people's ideas derive from and reflect their experience of everyday life *coupled with* the notions that, first, much of everyday life is spent in occupational roles and, second, that these occupational roles are created by the society's current industrial stage. If there are, for instance, ideas about the world which are typical to K Street lawyers, you will not likely encounter these ideas in a horticultural society which doesn't have anything like a K Street, let alone lawyers to walk along it, cell phones to their ears. The extension of Schutz's ideas about the salience of everyday life for idea formation specifically to the world of occupations has been addressed by Bensman and Lilienfeld.[15] They, however, take their analysis in rather a different direction.

In our view, the factors in a situation—including an occupational situation created by an individual's having that kind of a job— impacting the likelihood that particular ideas will be generated include the following:

- People tend to develop ideas compatible with, or which make sense of, their own situations. This can occur even when these ideas are not strictly compatible with their material interests (recall our example of businesspeople and deficit spending cited in a prior chapter).

- People tend to develop ideas that serve either their own personal interests or the interests of groups of which they are members. This is a species of the prior factor ("compatibility with their own situation"). Material interest is, after all, a kind of "compatibility."

14. *Ibid.*, pp. 15-17.

15. Joseph Bensman and Robert Lilienfeld, *Craft and Consciousness* (New York: Wiley-Interscience, 1973).

It is, however, so important in influencing people and so broadly recognized as impacting political ideology that we have segregated it out. Indeed, many people would assert that material interest is *always* behind and the basis for ideological pronouncements. We disagree with this extreme position.

- People tend to develop ideas that support the interests and perspectives of other groups which are, in one way or another, compatible or allied with the perspectives of one's own group. Such relationships are called "constituency relationships," and we shall frequently refer to them later in the book.

- People can also generate ideas that they are paid to generate and on behalf of some party who actually pays them to generate. This sort of creative thinking is done by advertising profession-als, public relations professionals, and attorneys. It is, obviously, a species—though a very distinct species—of influence by material interest. We shall refer to such relationships as "client" relationships.

Now, all these factors that predispose people to *create* an idea of a certain type *also predispose them to be receptive to these same types of ideas.* For example, if the experience of being a civil servant predisposes you to *imagine* that a large, activist federal government is a good thing, then being a civil servant will also predispose you to *accept* this kind of an idea even if you didn't think of it first.

There are, however—and in addition to those factors cited above—certain other factors predisposing a person to accept and/or retain ideas of a certain sort which are communicated to them from an external source:

- People tend to believe what those around them believe, and they believe it more strongly if there is a high level of homogeneity in one's own group regarding the idea in question. That is, the greater the uniformity of belief in your group as, for example, regards the idea that you shouldn't shoplift, the higher the probability that you will share this belief—and the higher the probability that you will not shoplift. The less the homogeneity—the more and varied the alternative patterns of belief and behavior with which life confronts you—the less powerfully held and motivating will be your own ideas about this kind of belief and behavior. This sort of "social pressure" to conform not only in behavior but in thought is particularly important in the study of ideology. It means, among other things, that a person who might be propelled, by his or her social position to believe one thing—but who lives in a community in which the predominant opinion is the opposite—is likely to conform with the community opinion.

- People will more readily accept and retain any particular idea if it is "moralized," that is, accompanied by an accessory idea that good or moral people are expected to subscribe to it. For instance, the idea that one should not shoplift becomes more readily accepted and powerfully retained if it is accompanied by a parallel idea that shoplifting is not simply against the law but immoral. The power to moralize an idea—to make subscription to it moral and rejection of it immoral—is a profound power. It can be used, for instance, to compensate for an idea's shaky factual basis: if believing an idea is a matter of morality—if rejecting it is a sin—then you can get away with some very weak factual argument. This suggests a hypothesis (deriving from the theory of cognitive dissonance) that—under conditions of ideology—the more morally-charged an argument is, the weaker the factual basis for that argument will be.

- People tend to believe what they are taught. This isn't very surprising, and it is more useful in accounting for how an idea stays in a culture once it has been introduced than accounting for how it enters the culture in the first place. We will not spend much time explaining why German-speaking people tend to believe that German verb conjugation should be done in accordance with the rules of conjugation for German; this sort of thing will be taken as a given. What is more important for our own purposes is that people—particularly young people—will learn ideologies from their elders even though they have not yet been exposed to the forces which play upon mature adults in the society. Therefore, insofar as young people move into societal roles similar to the roles of their parents, they will come ideologically prepared to function in and reflect those social roles.

- People tend to be receptive to ideas—as well as to other cultural forms like styles of dress and speech—mediated to them by high-status or otherwise aggrandized or esteemed people. Thus, we tend to buy the deodorant—or the political views—associated with a movie star or nationally known athlete not because he or she knows much about deodorants or politics, but because we admire the person (or, at least, we think that we ought to because all our friends do) whether consciously or unconsciously. Through this particular factor—as it is amplified *via* the electronic mass media—particular ideological themes and styles become matters of fashion. To call something a matter of "fashion" is to say that it is a popular or received thing to do or to wear or to believe or to possess. This factor is critical to the realization—in the contemporary American context—of Marx's dictum that any age's ruling ideas are those of its more powerful social groups. It is, thus, critical to any understanding of the phenomenon of "false consciousness."

To repeat, what we have reviewed here are the factors inducing individual people to either create and transmit ideas of a particular sort or to be receptive to ideas of this sort. In the earlier chapters we examined how the economy organizes the society we live in and how our social roles determine our experience as individuals. It is the combination of these three levels of analysis—economy/technology, society, and culture—that make our argument possible.

We would note, finally, that we have identified factors that propel people to both create and be receptive to ideas of certain sorts. For the most part, these factors predispose people to either generate or to accept ideas that either serve their own and their families' or group's interests or, in some other way, make sense of the world from their own perspective. The one important exception is the factor which we mentioned last—the tendency for people to accept ideas mediated to them from outside of their own groups and which have been given the patina of fashionability. For people to hold ideas reflecting their own group's position in the world is a normal state of affairs and, in general, good for those people. For people to accept group-alien ideas because they come to them *via* the mass media ornamented with the trappings of fashion is often bad for those people. This fact—that people's ideas may not reflect their own group's position in the world but that of another group with a very different set of circumstances and interests—is crucial. This condition, which proceeds from (indeed, it is nearly coextensive with) a condition of "false consciousness," is sufficiently important that we have devoted an entire section of Chapter XII to false consciousness and to coping therewith.

In Chapter XII we also address the problem of getting beyond thinking that reflects solely and simply either one's own perspective or the perspective of groups in a position of sufficient power to mediate their own ideological beliefs to large masses of people. We are persuaded that the most effective tools available to guide decision-making in a way which transcends both one's own and such powerful parties' versions of the "here and now" are metaphysical traditions of great venerability—principally philosophical or religious bodies of thought—which have evolved through history so as to have transcended many "heres" and many "nows" themselves.

B. THE MORALIZATION OF IDEOLOGY

Ideologies not only *describe* reality from a certain perspective, but they also *prescribe* that reality be seen and understood from that perspective, and they *proscribe* that it be seen and understood from other, incompatible, perspectives. In other words, ideology has a moral dimension, and the importance of this moral dimension—that "right ideology" distinguishes between good people and bad people—will be critical throughout the book. Unsurprisingly, the members of one's own group—one's "in-group"—will be perceived as having the "right" ideology, and members of the other groups—the out-groups—will be perceived as having the "wrong" ideology. And this difference between "right" and "wrong" ideologies—while it may have a descriptive component—is, for our purposes here, a moral difference: people who, ideologically speaking, subscribe to the "right" point of view are "morally good" people, and people who subscribe to the "wrong" point of view are "morally bad" people.

The connections between ideology, group affiliation, and morality are the bases for the power of the demagogue: the person who can identify in-groups and out-groups and—by using their skills of applying and manipulating ideology—paint the members of one group as morally good people and the members of the other as morally bad people.

Jonathan Rauch puts this connection in prehistorical perspective:

> Modern scholarship suggests that reasoning arose from a differ-
> ent imperative than raw survival: persuasion. People originally
> lived in small bands, or tribes. Survival depended on being able
> to win a secure place within the group for oneself and one's
> children. Being shunned, abandoned, or cast out could be fatal.
> In contrast, high status could bring resources and mating oppor-
> tunities. One way to gain dominance might be physical, by killing
> or overpowering competitors; but that path invites rivals to form
> alliances and to go to war. The gift of persuasion has lower costs
> and higher returns. With it, we can persuade others to follow
> where wish to go, to do what we prefer to do, to ally with us and
> protect us, and to provide us with aid and resources.[16]

Now, demagogues—those master persuaders—take advantage of our predisposition to moralize ideology to get their way, and they accomplish this by associating proper morality with in-group membership. Moreover, once minds get made up—minds grounded in group identity and the sort of moralization which attends group identity—they are highly impervious to change. Rausch again:

16. Jonathan Rauch, *The Constitution of Knowledge: A Defense of Truth* (Washington, D. C.: Brookings Institution Press, 2021), pp. 22-23.

... humans are equipped with some of evolution's finest mental circuitry to protect us from changing our minds when doing so might alienate us from our group. We have hundreds of thousands of years of practice at believing whatever will keep us in good standing with our tribe, even if that requires denying, discounting, rationalizing, misperceiving, and ignoring the evidence in front of our nose.[17]

So, one's ideology becomes a badge of belonging to a group or "tribe," and—more than that—a badge of virtue. And these two positive dimensions of the badge interact with and mutually support one another: One's affiliation with a particular tribe predicts and reinforces that one will subscribe to the right beliefs and celebrate the right totems ... and one's public allegiance to the proper beliefs and totems show that one is a member of one's chosen in-group.

The discussions one reads currently—and particularly in the literature of the American Right—about "virtue signaling" (identifying and mocking the assertion of statements of moralized ideology by Leftists) has it right, but only to a limited extent. A more even-handed treatment of virtue signaling would acknowledge that:

- The virtues being signaled are those of—and are being directed to—the members of a particular tribe *and not to everybody*.

- Both sides do it ... and with about equal frequency.

---

17. *Ibid.*, p. 32.

V. AMERICA AND THE AMERICAN CHARACTER

CONSIDER THE CASE OF THE LATE and somewhat apocryphal Mrs. X: born in 1900 somewhere in the American Mid-West, passed on to her reward in the year 2000. She was born into a world in which no airplane had ever flown, in which even the horseless carriage was still a novel device, a world in which an obscure young patent clerk in Switzerland was making private notes about the nature of matter, time, and energy ... notes which would, five years later, be published as the Theory of Relativity. In her girlhood she had, as all farm girls had, been assigned certain duties around the house and farm: in the mornings before school she and her sisters put the rigging on the horses so that the team would be ready for their father to work them, and, every Saturday, they trimmed the wicks of the kerosene lamps.

Quite a ride it was, twentieth-century America. Not everybody has had the constitutional robustness of a Mrs. X to have lived a hundred years, but any part of the twentieth century was a period of radical change. Mrs. X, in her time, saw:

- Economic and technological change, such as the advent of both human-powered flight and space travel, nuclear technology, and the computer (in fact, if Mrs. X were to have [until the mid-fifties] looked up "computer" in her dictionary she would have found that it meant "one who computes!"),

- Social change, e.g., the emergence of a new middle class, based in large organizations and living in urban and suburban settings,

- Cultural change: she grew up singing the popular songs of the early part of the century—songs with the cleverness of Cole Porter's *Anything Goes*, the sweetness of Paul Dresser's *On the Banks of the Wabash far Away, Moonlight in Vermont*: a *haiku* in song by John Blackburn and Karl Suessdorf; she died to the sounds of gangster rap.

Sic transit gloria mundi.

A. WHERE WE HAVE BEEN

We have noted earlier that the 1880 census marked an economic and demographic tipping-point at which most Americans were no longer employed on the farm. If one were to take this as a rough socio-historical milepost, then it represents the endpoint of a very long run for life based on horticulture or agriculture (and we distinguish horticulture from agriculture by the use of the plow in agriculture) which, in Europe, began at about the beginning of the Neolithic, some 4,000 years BC.

Certainly, our American agrarian ancestors got the best part of this eons-long agricultural era, coming with European agricultural technology into a land which had never been laid open by the plow. Moreover, the last century of this period—say, 1780 to 1880, the post-Colonial period—was a time when the benefits of early industrialization could be enjoyed by farm families and the small-town *petit bourgeoisie* families which supported the agricultural economy. Notwithstanding the wars and the depressions marking the period, this agrarian experience is remembered (at least by Americans of European ancestry and through the soft focus of memory) as a happy time. American culture still retains the stamp of this period in our appreciation of country and folk music and early Southern music of all sorts, an abiding attraction to rural scenery, and in our deepest personal aspirations: nobody dreams about hitting it big and moving to the suburbs.

The American agrarian period began with European settlement, in Colonial, pre-Revolutionary times, prior to the advent of the Industrial Revolution and lasted well into the nineteenth century. However, during a period spanning roughly 1780 to 1960—from the beginning of the Industrial Revolution to the beginning of the Service Economy—the old agrarian order was challenged and ultimately overcome—economically, socially, and culturally—by the new industrial order. With the advent of a powerful industrial technological base, the larger portion of contributed GNP began to shift from the farms and the farmers to the factories and to the newly emergent urban bourgeoisie. Regionally, this marked a period of ascendancy for the northeastern part of the nation and particularly for the urban northeast. Socially and politically, the classes based upon this new economic order, and led by the interests of the grand bourgeoisie, came to determine the policies pursued by the federal government. Midway through the nineteenth century, the collision between the interests of northeastern industrialists and southeastern agriculturists and incidentally involving the institution of race slavery in the agrarian south reached a peak, the collision resolving itself through the pursuit of the American Civil War and the defeat of southern agrarian separatism.

The social institutions characterizing the old order reflected their agricultural economic base. Extended families were based on the need for farm labor and upon the inheritance of that one inexorably immovable resource: land. Social life was organized into very local institutions—churches, town councils, sewing circles—because the technologies of transportation and communication were, relative to what came later, impuissant. And, above all, everything was small, small because agriculture cannot, by itself, support as many people on a unit of land as can manufacturing industry. In 1900 the population of the United States was 76 million, less than a quarter of its present size.

That time's culture—particularly from the early part of this period—comes to us best through its literature, accepting that the culture of those producing literature is not the culture of the masses. The heroic figures—Melville's Starbuck or Mark Twain's Huckleberry Finn—are driven by very old sensibilities about what is right and proper. Music is largely homemade and derived from the ethnic traditions of the families whose hands and voices made it. Public morality, including sexual morality and beliefs about property, came from a Judeo-Christian tradition which was already at least a thousand years old among these tribes. Our people were, as are rural people everywhere, narrow and deep.

In the culture, the growth of the new socioeconomic groups based in secondary industry produced changes which conflicted with the culture of the agrarian time. Really bad jokes became "corny" jokes ... because they and their raconteurs came from the areas where corn was grown. The images of the yeoman farmer or the sturdy small-town merchant came to be transformed in the public imagination to the images of "hick," "hayseed," "bumpkin" and Babbitt. Images of White southerners, in particular—tied as they were to the Civil War, poverty, and an agricultural region—deteriorated, though not as sharply as they would in the subsequent period. In the motion pictures of the talking era, the most exemplary American figures come to be Spencer Tracy, Katherine Hepburn, Humphrey Bogart: whether middle class or working class, their characters are smart, both urban and urbane, vaguely northeastern (the "Mid-Atlantic Accent"), their voices quick, taut and sharp.

Without endeavoring to create a cultural history of the first two centuries of the Republic, we would argue that the most important social changes marking this 1780-1960 period were the emergence and ultimately the social dominance of classes or occupational categories based on manufacturing industry and that the social emergence and dominance of these groups is only explicable and comprehensible in terms of the development of industrial technology: steam power, internal combustion, electricity, modern metallurgy, etc. Absent these critical technologies—or their functional equivalents (other technologies which might have permitted similar levels of manufacturing productivity during this period)—the American culture of the time would have been very different. We would argue, beyond this, that part of the culture came to be the signs of the very conflict between the old agrarian order and the emerging industrial order: the images of in-groups and out-groups dominant in the popular culture, the emergence of a Republican northeast opposed by a solidly Democratic south, the ascendancy of national and international views over parochial views and all the rest.

To choose the year 1960 as the beginning of the new time is at least a little bit arbitrary. 1945 is a good candidate, too, simply because it marks the end of World War II and the development of very early versions of the electronic computer. Or 1981 because it marks the release of the first mass-produced personal computer. We have chosen 1960 because it marks the beginning of a period of prosperity based on service-sector growth and the election of a new president, a conservative Democrat, whose assassination would bring into office a successor who would, working from precedents established during the New Deal, amplify the power and presence of that largest of all service providers: the US federal government.

Services and computers: they are not the same thing, and one does not necessarily imply the use or provision of the other, but they bear a certain mutual complementarity in the new economy. Certainly, specialized services have been provided since deep in the Paleolithic: shamanism is (contrary to conventional wisdom) probably the oldest profession … and, to be sure, prostitution is a specialized service in its own right. And computers can be used to detonate charges, operate equipment, or do any number of very mechanical things. Still, the essence of a service is that it has neither weight nor volume but is still scarce and useful; the essence of a computer is that it processes information, and information is one of the very few substances that has neither weight nor volume but is still scarce and useful. So, the computer is, as a technology, critical to the service-based economy into which the United States' economy has been transformed over the past six decades. Admiral Hyman Rickover oversaw the nuclear propulsion development program for the US Navy. He described this program as being much more of a management challenge than a technological challenge, and it was met in the 1950s mostly without the aid of computers but with enormously complex and meticulous manual information management systems. Thus, in the few decades prior to the incorporation of computers into the economy, sophisticated information-processing systems of manual and electro-mechanical sorts were available to those who needed them and had the power to command their use.

In fact, history is a process and not sequenced sets of events, but we've got a book to write, and it's enormously more convenient to both reader and author to be able to point to two separate "eras" or "phases" than to refer to different moments in a process. This said, we shall begin with a nominal date of 1960 in the next chapter and consider, by application of the theoretical framework which we have developed in the earlier chapters, what our country has become.

B. DAVID RIESMAN: "SOCIAL CHARACTER" AND SOCIAL STRUCTURE

Now, we've developed, in the prior chapters, a basic theory relating these kinds of things—ideology, social structure, and economy—with one another, and, if the reader has been at all persuaded, he or she should have the sense that all of these different kinds of phenomena are connected in some knowable, comprehensible, way. It is, at this juncture, useful to enlist the aid of David Riesman. Reisman's training was as an attorney, but his very considerable career derived from his writings on society, beginning, particularly, with the publication, in 1950, of *The Lonely Crowd*. The core notion of the book is that "social character"—which Reisman defines as "... that part of 'character' which is shared among significant social groups and which, as most contemporary social scientists define it, is the product of the experience of these groups."[18]—is determined by the era in which people live.

Riesman creates a typology of social character types and associates them with particular phases in economic development. In fact, we will use our own labels for these phases because Riesman's phraseology, in the original text, derives from the population-growth characteristics accompanying these industrial phases and is, we believe, confusing (and which Riesman himself very strongly de-emphasizes in the *Preface* to the 1961 edition).[19]

---

18. David Riesman with Nathan Glazer and Reuel Denney, *The Lonely Crowd* (New Haven and London: Yale University Press, 1961), p. 4.

19. *Ibid.*, p. xxx.

FIGURE 2. DAVID RIESMAN'S MODEL OF THE RELATIONSHIP BETWEEN SOCIAL CHARACTER AND INDUSTRIAL PHASE

CHARACTER TYPE	INDUSTRIAL PHASE	DOMINANT INDUSTRY TYPE (Our Addition)
Tradition-Directed: The individual bases his or her behavior upon obedience to age-old cultural traditions.	**Pre-industrial**	**Primary**
Inner-Directed: The individual bases his or her behavior upon beliefs which are instilled into the individual very early in life by his or her elders and directed toward generalized goals.	**Industrial**	**Secondary**
Other-Directed: The individual bases his or her behavior upon his or her observation of others and is guided into conformity with them.	**Post-Industrial**	**Tertiary**

Riesman supports the idea that the experience of life in societies based on economies of corresponding sorts gives rise to these characteristic character types. Examples of the types are familiar, whether from personal experience or from literature:

- **The Tradition-Directed person**—exemplified by Chingach-gook, Cincinnatus, Dersu Uzala—is a sort of a noble savage: noble because the beliefs governing his or her activities come from the ancestors and are unquestioned and because only in a relatively simple and slow-changing society can such beliefs go unchallenged by alternative ways of believing ... and "savage" because they take these ideas seriously.

- **The Inner-Directed person**—exemplified by Henry Ford, Thomas Edison, Theodore Roosevelt, or Albert Einstein—is oriented toward achievement of goals in a world populated prominently by material objects. For this person directed by religious values inculcated early in life, the world, in both its human and non-human elements, is to be manipulated in accordance with these values in support of the achievement of these goals.

- **The Other-Directed person**—exemplified by ... anybody who has ever gone through a Sensitivity Training program and had it take ... anybody who is brought to tears (of sympathy, not of laughter) by guests on the Oprah Winfrey Show. The other-directed person is steered by the actions and signals of others, principally because he or she lives in a socially dense world; he or she—there in his or her cubicle—doesn't manipulate things; he or she manipulates people and information about people, and that takes *sensitivity*.

The other aspect of Riesman's work in *The Lonely Crowd* that makes him so useful for us is that he is talking about the United States, and he is chiefly discussing the twentieth century. He doesn't spend much time with tradition-direction because he sees it as a feature of an historically and socially earlier age. His real interest was—writing in the period just after World War II—the transition from inner-direction to other-direction. And this is why his book came to be so widely read and so very important in the informed discourse of the 1950s: Americans had the sense that things were changing—that *they themselves* were changing—and that there was something aesthetically or morally disagreeable about these changes. Writing in the *Preface* to the 1960 edition, Riesman refers to what had been the popular reaction to the book over the intervening ten years:

> ... the great majority of readers in the last ten years have decided that it was better to be an inner-directed cowboy than an other-directed advertising man, for they were not on the whole being faced with the problems of the cowboy, but rather those of the advertising man.[20]

In subsequent chapters we are going to look at America again—seventy years hence—and consider where we have come, beginning with where we have come from ... and we will not so much try to apply Riesman *in toto* to our time as to go armed with his ideas as well as others about social character and social structure in support of our own more general model of how things work.

---

20. *Ibid.*, pp. xvii-xviii.

SECTION TWO:

THE YEOMANY AND THE COGNOSCENTI

VI. THE YEOMANY, THE COGNOSCENTI, AND FORMAL ORGANIZATION

IN THE FOREGOING CHAPTERS—WHICH COMPRISE Section One of the book—we have offered a sociology of knowledge: more precisely, a sociology of ideology. We have described the evolution of American society from the nineteenth century to the twenty-first century, and we have reviewed David Riesman's triality of Tradition-Directed, Inner-Directed, and Other-Directed social characters. It is now time to apply these more generalized ideas to the contemporary American social scene (though these ideas will apply, *mutatis mutandis*, to the developed world more generally) and its painfully apparent ideological divisions and to tailor and adapt them to that scene and its divisions.

Certainly, the most apparent division in the nation currently is between those who voted for Donald Trump in the 2016 and 2020 presidential elections and those who did not (and there were more than eleven million more of the former in 2020 than in 2016). One might be tempted, therefore—and in order to develop a useful nomenclature—to refer to the two groups as "Trumpers" and "Anti-Trumpers," or something of the sort, but there are several reasons to avoid so doing. The first—and most important—is that the forces that Trump came to mobilize and symbolize predated Trump and will succeed him. Related to that is the fact that to dwell on Trump as a symbol will conceal these actual forces at work ... and the former president is much more a symptom than a cause. Another is that naming groups for an American figure will be incompatible with any generalization to other societies. Finally, Trump, as an historical figure, is simply too fundamentally flawed to in any way further memorialize him.

So, given that the purpose of this portion of the book is to account for the existence and character of these two contesting and opposed groups, we must create some nomenclature for the sake of convenience, and a nomenclature which will be relevant for the theory explaining the differences between their characteristic ideologies.

It is best, therefore, to begin with a summary statement of that theory.

We are going to argue that the best way to account for ideological differences across the American political divide is by the relationship that individual people have to formal organizations.

What are formal organizations? For our purposes, we are going to say that *formal organizations are social organizations which are deliberately established for specific purposes.* Both characteristics are important. A formal organization must be *deliberately established*: for example, a group of founders might establish and incorporate a software development firm, or a government department might establish, furnish, fund, and staff a new office. In both cases the new organizations are the products of deliberate establishment. Secondly, these two new organizations are established with *specific purposes* in mind: in the first case, the founders are creating the new firm in order, say, to develop enterprise management software, sell the software, and make a profit; in the second case, a department of public safety might establish a new office with the specific purpose of advancing community policing.

Formal organizations are contrasted with non-formal or "traditional" social organizations such as families and communities. Such organizational forms are much older in human history and pre-history than are formal organizations. Traditional organizations emerge out of the mists of time and are more governed by unwritten social norms than by laws and written rules (though, in the modern context, laws are written to govern some aspects of, for example, families and communities). The norms governing such traditional organizations are conveyed, from generation to generation, by families and by the organizations themselves. The specific normative structures controlling behavior in traditional organizations will, of course, vary by culture; this is part of what makes them traditional. One might rejoin that "Well, when two people decide to get married and then get married, don't they deliberately establish that social organization?" They deliberately get married, but the purposes of a marriage are anything but specific: the partners pledge to support one another for richer, for poorer, for better, for worse, in sickness and in health 'til death us do part. Moreover, when children are born into that marriage—and children turn a couple into a family—they have no say at all as to the purposes of the organization. It's the same with communities: you move into a community for a job, say, but then you meet neighbors and other people and—through interaction with them—establish friendship groups, bowling leagues, the girls down at Hadassah, etc.

So, the rules governing behavior in formal and traditional organizations are very different. In formal organizations the rules are written down: either externally as a matter of law or internally, as a matter of organizational governance policy. In a corporation there will be by-laws and an employee handbook as well as extensive organizational policy documents. If you are at a loss to know how to behave in a certain situation, you can look it up—or you can go to a designated policy specialist to consult on the matter. And—if you fail to follow written policy—you can be sanctioned. In a traditional organization the governance of behavior is accomplished by norms rather than written rules. In families there are shared understandings about what constitutes a good mom or a good dad. In communities there are norms about not being a jerk, not being a slacker. For almost the entirety of the three hundred thousand-year experience of *Homo sapiens* on the planet,[21] all but the last six thousand years (and, for most of our ancestors, *much* more recently than that), traditional organizations and their unwritten norms were the *only* experience of social life that humans had. To call them "traditional" doesn't mean that they are either unimportant or *passé*.

Now, for individual humans, the subjective experience of everyday life in formal and traditional organizations is very different. Human beings live—and, as a social species, always have lived—most of their waking hours in social organizations and not in isolated settings. While formal and traditional organizations are both social, humans rub up against life very differently in the two. Because formal organizations are deliberately established for specific purposes, the rules governing behavior in them are products of rational deliberation. *Indeed, formal organizations may be regarded as being the social embodiment of rationality itself.* Even when rules in a formal organization are encountered (as they often are) which are outmoded, arbitrary or just plain dumb, such encounters are the product of rationality encountering rules that fail to measure up by a standard of rationality. Such encounters are what lead, optimally, to changes in formal organizations. Thus, the subjective encounter with life in formal organizations is an encounter with rationality itself, with processes and

---

21. Reich, *loc. cit.*

procedures designed to facilitate the goals of the organization. There are, of course, friendship groups which form within the workplace, so that the experience is not unadulterated, but the operating precept of the formal organization is the rational pursuit of the goals of the organization. Just like the rules, the individuals staffing a formal organization have been deliberately selected for specific purposes. They are selected based upon their expertise for a position, and—if they fail to discharge the duties associated with that position—they will be dismissed and replaced with some other person. Likewise, if, due to some organizational change, the position disappears, the person does as well.

The experience of an individual in a traditional organization is very different. Because the rules governing behavior are unwritten traditional norms, these rules—while effective—are less intrusive into the individual's consciousness. Unlike the rules in a formal organization, rules in a traditional organization are not normally pondered; such rules possess the power of apparent obviousness, unanimity, and venerability. The rules in a traditional organization enjoy the quiet force of defining the single and unchallenged way a good person might behave. The rules will vary among traditional categories of person: males versus females, child versus adult, married versus unmarried. Whereas formal organizations exist for the pursuit of their specific and stated goals, the traditional organization's "goal" is the very existence of the organization itself. Involvement in a traditional organization—a family, a community, a friendship group, a religious group—is emotionally much more engaging than in a formal organization. Accordingly, separation—other than by death—from a traditional organization is emotionally much more wrenching for the separated individual than dismissal from a formal organization. To be shunned by your family, or your friends or your co-religionists is a very painful experience. Likewise, an individual's death is cause for emotional outpouring and memorialization by those remaining in the traditional organization. Membership in traditional organizations—for the intensely social and self-aware species that is *Homo sapiens*—gives meaning to life: "I *am* a mom"; "I *am* a friend."

Finally, we propose that people (other than those under duress or sanction) understand their own life experience to be the normal and acceptable life experience. Thus, people are parochial in the sense that they understand the everyday life experiences of themselves and people like themselves to be what human life is normally and properly like. It follows, therefore, that people who live their lives in formal organizations will have a very different view of what constitutes a normal and acceptable life than will people—even in the same society—who do not.

Now, we began this chapter with a foray into nomenclature, veering off into a contrast of formal and traditional organization as theoretical objects with an implicit promise to bring these two lines of conversation together. It is time to make good on that promise. We shall argue that the principal political and ideological division in the United States is between two groups who have different relationships to formal organization. We will say that there exists a:

- **Yeomanry**—consisting of Americans who spend more time in—and take their most important social statuses from—traditional organizations, and a

- **Cognoscenti**—consisting of Americans who spend more time inside (and not at the periphery) of—and take their most important social statuses from—formal organizations.

Why these particular terms?

"The yeomanry" is, as a term, used much more in connection with British history than with the American present. In British history the yeomanry were—and are—holders of small landed estates. The term is also used to refer to units of the British military raised from this part of British society. The elements of both rurality, property ownership, and involvement in the national military seem to ring true with the Americans whom we wish to discuss under this rubric, and, so—and rather than resort to some silly neologism—"yeomanry" it is.

And the cognoscenti. In popular discourse "cognoscenti" (singular: cognoscente) refers to a group of people with expertise in a particular subject. This seemed to be appropriate for people who staff formal organizations based on their expertise (as Max Weber characterized members of a bureaucracy). Also, we thought that they'd like the Italianate flair of the term.

Now, what—as constructs and in the context of mainstream sociological thinking—*are* the yeomanry and the cognoscenti? In sociological thought all but the simplest societies are stratified—or "layered"—and the most common systems have generally been characterized as being caste, estate, or class systems of stratification.

Among these three, class is probably the most likely candidate in that the traditional dimensions of class are wealth, power, and prestige, and certainly—on every one of these dimensions—the cognoscenti, collectively, outrank the yeomanry. However, there are a couple of problems with casting this effort into a class stratification format. First, features of the yeomanry/cognoscenti distinction—for instance geography and rurality/urbanity and particularly relationship to formal organization—are not captured in conventional treatments of class systems of stratification. Second—and particularly because of Marx' importance in the early sociology of knowledge—calling the yeomanry/cognoscenti divide a class divide will almost automatically invite a Marxist analysis of this current division, *and the analysis here provided will not be a Marxist analysis.* In Marxian analyses classes are *functional;* they drive history. Remember: "The history of all hitherto existing society is the history of class struggles." This analysis will not go down that particular analytical rathole.

In any event, we shall refer to the yeomanry and the cognoscenti as *sectors*—a nice, theoretically agnostic term—within American society and not as classes, castes, or estates. In addition, the term "sector" does not imply stratification—which denotes inequality with respect to one another—at all. What the idea of "sector" does accommodate, though, is stratification *within* each of the two sectors, and there is, of course, stratification by wealth, power and prestige within both sectors.

A. MEET THE YEOMANRY

The American yeomanry consists of that sector of American society which has been *least* transformed by the post–World War II industrial revolution which metamorphosed the society from one based chiefly upon primary (extractive) industry and secondary (manufacturing) industry to a society based principally upon producing and delivering services, which is called "tertiary industry." It is the nature of tertiary industry to produce large formal organizations, and formal organizations of a particular sort. While manufacturing—and to a lesser extent, extractive—industries can often produce large formal organizations, their organizations have large "peripheral areas," i.e., participants not clearly embedded in the organization in the sense that their work for the organization is with the things the organization produces and not with the way the organization functions internally. These "peripheral" workers—think of workers on a factory floor—work more with things than they do with people. Workers more deeply embedded in the organization work not with things but with information: symbols of things ... and, of course, with people. One might consider this a blue collar/white collar distinction, though there is more to the American yeomanry than blue-collar workers.

The large formal organizations created by tertiary industry are, by contrast, almost completely white collar. Very few people work with things. Almost everybody works with symbols of things, i.e., information ... and, of course, with people. And contemporary large service organizations—whether public or private sector—can be very large, indeed. Tens of millions of Americans spend their waking hours processing information in social settings. These are the cognoscenti.

The yeomanry cited as examples above are the people who dwell, occupationally, away from these centers of information processing. They may work for formal organizations but only on the outside. They leave the construction job, the factory floor, the mine, the road crew, and head home at the end of the day with empty lunch pails. Often, though, the yeomanry are self-employed farmers, tradesmen, or craftsmen and small business owners, all of whom have little contact with large formal organizations. An auto repair shop may have been deliberately established for specific purposes, but it has very little "middle" and a lot of periphery: In most cases the shop owner still pulls wrenches.

The key characteristic, then, of the yeomanry isn't being blue-collar, *per se*; rather, it is having a connection to large formal organizations which may be described as attenuated. While they may be employed by large organizations, they work on the peripheries of such organizations, and they work with things rather than purely with information: metaphorically, they work *for* the formal organization rather than *in* it. In an important sense they have been bypassed by recent history inasmuch as the "information economy" that burgeoned in the seven decades after

World War II missed them and, indeed, came to alienate them.

There is information in the work that they do—in some cases quite a lot. Tool and die maker, seamstress, plumber, all of these require a lot of specialized knowledge. But this specialized knowledge comes not from science or organizational policy but from craft, and craft is information accumulated by generations of practitioners. It is knowledge based upon job experience and the creative ideas of the people who did those jobs and passed on those ideas to those who followed in the trade.

Science, by contrast—and, in particular, that quintessentially scientific practice, the experiment—is concentrated, accelerated, and rationally designed experience. Not all science can be experimental, but all science relies on systematic observation and the recording and analysis of data. In no other field of human endeavor is the adjective "anecdotal" a slur. Craft grows linearly; science grows exponentially as do the technologies which rely upon science.

The attenuated relationship the yeomanry has to large formal organizations also brings with it a geographic dimension. Such large formal organizations tend to cluster in urban areas, many of them on the Atlantic and Pacific coasts of America. Such areas are, accordingly, areas dominated by the cognoscenti, not the yeomanry. The yeomanry dwell in the small towns and rural areas—"flyover country"—and in urban areas only insofar as there are manufacturing industries there.

Since we are defining the yeomanry primarily upon the basis of occupation, it is worthwhile to consider the demographic size of the yeomanry. In 2021 the size of the civilian, non-institutionalized US workforce was approximately 162 million Americans.[22] Of these:

---

22. US Bureau of Labor Statistics, *Employment status of the civilian population by sex and age* (US Bureau of Labor Statistics, accessed 2022), https://www.bls.gov/news.release/empsit.t01.htm

- About ten million were self-employed.[23]

- About thirty-two million were small business owners.[24]

- About twenty-three million were blue-collar.[25]

- And about two million were farmers.[26]

This totals to about sixty-seven million Americans—not quite half, particularly given the possibility of double counting in these data from multiple sources—constituting the basis, occupationally defined, of the American yeomanry in recent years. This is a substantial proportion (about 41 percent) of the American workforce and, thus potentially, of the American electorate. It is, however, smaller than the proportion of the electorate (about 47 percent) which voted for Trump in 2020. What might explain this difference?

Most importantly, the vote totals—and, thus, the presidential vote percentages—reflect not only the votes of the yeomanry and the cognoscenti but of their respective ideological constituencies as well. Moreover, the ideological constituencies of the cognoscenti are much more numerous than the ideological constituencies of the yeomanry. The nature of ideological constituencies will be considered in detail later in the book.

23. _____ , *Selected Employment Indicators* (US Bureau of Labor Statistics, accessed 2022), https://www.bls.gov/webapps/legacy/cpsatab9.htm

24. US Small Business Administration, Office of Advocacy, *Frequently Asked Questions* (US Small Business Administration, accessed 2022), https://cdn.advocacy.sba.gov/wp-content/uploads/2020/11/05122043/Small-Business-FAQ-2020.pdf

25. Workable, *Blue Collar Worker Definition* (Workable, accessed 2022), https://resources.workable.com/hr-terms/blue-collar-worker-definition#:~:text=For%20example%2C%20in%202018%2C%20construction,are%20in%20blue%20collar%20professions

26. US Department of Agriculture, Economic Research Service, Farming and Farm Income (UDSA, accessed 2022), https://www.ers.usda.gov/data-products/ag-and-food-statistics-charting-the-essentials/farming-and-farm-income/#:~:text=Since%20then%2C%20the%20number%20of,from%202.2%20million%20in%202007

In addition, some of this difference is explained by a pattern of residence. A substantial majority of Americans (61 percent) live in places of fifty thousand residents or fewer.[27] This non-urban character of the American population is seldom discussed; indeed, it is easy to miss in American popular culture. The popular culture flows from—and the bulk of the wealth resides in—urban areas. Consider:

> The less-than-500 counties that Hillary Clinton carried nationwide [in 2016] encompassed a massive 64 percent of America's economic activity as measured by total output in 2015. By contrast, the more-than-2,600 counties that Donald Trump won generated just 36 percent of the country's output—just a little more than one-third of the nation's economic activity.[28]

This demographic residential pattern leads to situations in which many Americans who would—by virtue of their occupations—be in the ranks of the cognoscenti reside in communities dominated by a yeomanry culture. For example, a teacher living in a small community in Missouri will be surrounded by neighbors—neighbors she likes, neighbors whose children she might teach—who are yeomen and yeowomen either by virtue of their occupation or by the proliferation of local institutions—traditional social organizations—in small towns. She may be married to a yeoman; spouses tend to gravitate toward similar ideological positions. Eitan Hirsch observes that:

27. Amel Toukabri and Lauren Medina, *America: A Nation of Small Towns* (US Census bureau, 2020), https://www.census.gov/library/stories/2020/05/america-a-nation-of-small-towns.html

28. Mark Muro and Sifan Liu, *Another Clinton-Trump Divide: High-Output America vs. Low-Output America* (The Brookings Institution, 2016), https://www.brookings.edu/blog/the-avenue/2016/11/29/another-clinton-trump-divide-high-output-america-vs-low-output-america/

First, 30 percent of married households contain a mismatched partisan pair. A third of those are Democrats married to Republicans. The others are partisans married to independents.[29]

These sorts of socially pressuring situations may be expected to move many people toward the community's ideological consensus.

B. MEET THE COGNOSCENTI

You probably know one. The cognoscenti tend to read books like this, though that's not their distinguishing trait. The distinguishing trait of the cognoscenti is that they spend their lives—or the occupational portion of their lives—in formal organizations. Such organizations may be corporate, governmental, academic, medical, non-profit, and so on. The characteristic these organizations share is that they are large enough to have a substantial portion of their workforce engaged in some information-processing function, or—even if small—they are primarily oriented toward information processing; i.e., information processing (including people processing) is their mission. This information processing needn't involve a computer—though a workstation graces almost every desk in a modern workspace—it must just involve the worker applying his or her expertise to the organization's informational needs. And all of these "bureaucratic" jobs involve some expertise. Whether it involves processing financial reports, editing proposals, developing Human Resources policy, every position requires some level of expertise requiring specialized training.

Not all skills in the positions in these organizations require higher education but many do, and the high number of university-educated

---

29. Eitan Hirsch, *How many Republicans Marry Democrats?* (FiveThirtyEight, 2016), https:// fivethirtyeight.com/features/how-many-republicans-marry-democrats/

workers in these organizations gives the entire organizational culture a white-collar complexion.

The cognoscenti spend their working hours in a social setting which is rationally designed for some purpose or purposes, a setting which can be readjusted, expanded, eliminated, recreated at any time; it is eternally and almost infinitely mutable. This doesn't mean that these individuals necessarily live in fear of losing their jobs, but it does mean that they live their lives in social roles obviously created for some reason. Both the yeomanry and the cognoscenti live their lives in social worlds which are man-made, but—in the case of the cognoscenti—this is much more obviously so.

Moreover, as was the case with the yeomanry, the cognoscenti are not only geographically situated in particular areas of the country, but also concentrated with others like themselves. The cognoscenti—like the yeomanry—sort themselves into communities primarily of their own kind.

And, critically, just as the yeomanry encounter a traditional world made up of traditional social organizations which have the appearance of immutability which durability in time confers, the cognoscenti encounter a world made up of formal social organizations which are infinitely mutable, rationally establishable, changeable at will. And—equally critically—each party regards that kind of world as normal ... because, of course, for them it is.

This experience of working purely with information inside of large formal organizations isn't historically unique: surely, there have been clerks, secretaries, and managers throughout the twentieth century and before. However, during the twentieth century and extending on into the twenty-first century, such occupations became a predominating portion of the American workforce. Thus, it is historically unique that such a large proportion of the society consists of people who take one of their most important statuses in life—if not the most important status—from their incumbency in a role in a social organization, a formal organization, which is so explicitly and obviously man-made. The everyday experience of life in such a social milieu is a practicum in the truth that all human social organization is man-made. It is man-made and can be remade by man on the basis of whatever rational—or apparently rational—bases are available. And—if social organization is artificial—that artifice may be fixed if it is broken, or its work might be done better. Indeed, it *should* be fixed; why not?

Because many of the necessary skills and expertise in modern formal organizations require university education, the cognoscenti are—relative to the yeomanry—more highly formally educated, and a greater proportion of the cognoscenti have university degrees and post-graduate degrees. With such levels of education and employment comes income such that the cognoscenti are, in general, wealthier than the yeomanry.

Now, when people with a view of the world as being man-made and inherently fixable look out at the rest of society, what they see is … positively Hobbesian! It's a mess! A mess ripe for fixing! Correspondingly, when the yeomanry looks back at the cognoscenti, they see a group of highly educated, wealthy, urbane people who think that they're a mess. And who act like it, too.

VII. THE IDEOLOGY OF
THE COGNOSCENTI

IN THE PREVIOUS CHAPTER WE have described the cognoscenti and the yeomanry socially, in terms of their roles and organizational affiliations, and related the evolution of those roles and organizations to changes in the economy—particularly as the economy has evolved in response to technological changes.

We turn now to the business of relating the ideologies of the cognoscenti and the yeomanry to the organizational roles in their respective lives. There are three issues here:

- First, there is the issue of who produces the ideologies that resonate with groups within this populace.

- Second, there is the question of what—in the experience of a life of a particular sort—predisposes a person to be receptive to an ideology of a certain sort.

- Finally, there is the matter of how ideologies become badges of affiliation with certain groups, how ideologies become "fashion accessories."

The first two points will be dealt with here for the cognoscenti and in the following chapter for the yeomanry. The last point will be touched on here but will be dealt with in greater detail in Chapter IX.

As this volume is being written, the occupational lives of the cognoscenti, in particular, but the yeomanry, as well, are emerging from—after having been profoundly impacted by—the COVID-19 pandemic. Specifically, people working with information—the cognoscenti—are opting to (in some cases being directed to) work remotely from home to minimize transmission of the disease. The typical cognoscenti home will have one or more internet-connected computers, and much of the information-based work of the individual cognoscente can be done *via* his or her home computer—or an employer-furnished computer—linked into their employer's digital enterprise. Some employees visit their physical office a few times a month … some not at all. A carpenter, by contrast, can't "call it in."

Indeed, the social effects of the COVID-19 pandemic will be wide and long-lasting. We can only now discern the largest of them. In addition to working from home, Americans very seldom use cash for economic transactions; they are used to purchasing online rather than going to brick-and-mortar retail shops; they are used to wearing masks in social settings, and none of this is likely to disappear coincidentally with the ultimate taming of the pandemic. Intriguingly, many Americans have simply left their jobs and produced a consequent labor shortage.

Remote work began as a prophylactic response to the pandemic, but few believe that it will end abruptly—if at all—when the pandemic ends. The benefits for both employers and employees have been substantial. Employers have realized an opportunity to significantly reduce their office-space costs. Employees have substantially reduced the cost and time of their commute and have gained much more flexibility over the use of their daytime hours.

Because we have argued that the ideological characteristics of the cognoscenti derive from their experience in formal organization, it may fairly be asked how this increased work from home will impact these ideological characteristics. The first—and very legitimate—answer is that we don't have any data yet, so we don't know with any certainty. That said, one might venture the hypothesis—based on the theory offered here—that working from home doesn't change the properties of work in formal organization; it merely changes their venue. The organizations—and the roles within them—are still formal in that they have been deliberately established for specific purposes. If the experience of life in such organizations is what drives cognoscenti ideology—*and if that life experience is substantially the same while working from home*—then working from home will not change that ideology.

A. THE CREATORS OF COGNOSCENTI IDEOLOGY

The cognoscenti are distinguished—ideologically speaking—by their *receptivity* to ideological themes particular to their group, a receptivity created by the social structural conditions determining their life experience … but a receptivity to ideology is not the same thing as producing that ideology. Most people don't go about their lives creating ideology; rather, they select from the ideas to which the culture exposes them and opt for those which make the most sense given their own life experience and which are endorsed and supported by those around them, in this case, other cognoscenti.

So, who produces the ideological thematic material for the cognoscenti? Multiple institutions, but prominent among them is the academy, and—more specifically—the departments of the social sciences and humanities. The role which such academic departments play in the creation of cognoscenti ideology is, indeed, overdetermined. Not only are universities and their constituent departments and offices formal organizations in and of themselves, the academics in these departments have a particular relationship to human social relations. Social scientists are abundantly aware that human social relationships are created by humans and vary according to the social order in which they occur. They are occasionally hired as consultants to facilitate change in social relationships in both formal organizations and in what have historically been traditional organizations. Humanities faculty—particularly writers of poetry and fiction—are literally in the business of creating literary models of social relationships. Again, they are professionally aware of the artificial nature of these relationships: they are the artists who portray them. Such academics are, therefore, not merely cognoscenti; they are among the most cognizant of all the cognoscenti. And, of course, they teach students and publish books and articles.

Another important source for the development of cognoscenti ideology is the "progressive" media—especially the opinion pages, though, to a lesser extent and chiefly with regard to choice of topic, the news pages as well. Reporters find themselves in an awkward and conflicted situation. They are—obviously, and by virtue of their work situation—cognoscenti themselves. They are, however, pledged to one level or another of a standard of fair and professional reporting by both a code of journalistic ethics and the norms of sound journalistic practice.

Political leaders would seem to be a natural source of ideological material, but—in the present case, at least—they seem to be much more ideologically reactive than proactive. Consider the Republican congressional caucus, for example. While many of them privately profess disgust for former president Trump, they toe his line (which largely involves the expression of personal loyalty) out of fear of their base voters, i.e., the yeomanry. And Trump is, of course, hardly a source of ideas.

These and other sources of *ideas deliberately and consciously created about human relationships*—Hollywood, and other creators of video drama, etc.—generate a stream of potential ideological themes for the cognoscenti, and the individual cognoscente will pick up those which resonate best with his or her own experience. Thus, while the social worker, the accountant, the public affairs officer do not generate much in the way of ideology, they find themselves with a rich and constant stream of ideas from which to select ... and their common life experience causes them to select similar ideas from this stream.

The creators of cognoscenti ideology are, in summary, culture-producing organizations. They produce ideas; they produce images; they produce the popular and broadly mediated culture of the nation.

B. THE IDEOLOGICAL CONSTITUENCIES OF THE COGNOSCENTI

Now, in Section C which follows, we will address which ideological themes appeal to and are articulated by the cognoscenti and how these themes reflect the social positions and experiences of the cognoscenti. However, prior to that it will be useful to broach the notion of "ideological constituency" as that notion will be referred to in the following section and the next chapters.

Any group will advocate for its own *ideological* interests—which is a very different thing, as we have shown, than advocating for its own *material* interests, the latter a being subset of the former. In addition, groups will advocate for (or against) *groups other than their own whose characteristics engage the ideology of the advocating group*. Such is the case with both the cognoscenti and the yeomanry (which we shall address later). Such groups selected for advocacy we shall call *ideological constituencies.*

The selection of an ideological constituency is seldom—perhaps never—a deliberate choice. Rather, it is an unconscious and collective choice of another group as a constituency because advocacy for that group is compatible with advancing the ideological position of the advocating group. By "advancing the ideological position," we mean that *such advocacy will help make the world more like the world as the advocating group experiences it.*

In the case of the cognoscenti—the social sector defined by its close relationship with formal organization—this will involve the subliminal selection of ideological constituencies advocacy for which will make the world more formalized, i.e., more like a formal organization. *Now, because formal organizations are deliberately established for specific purposes, making the world more like a formal organization will involve a deliberate intervention in the world's affairs to achieve specific goals.* Such deliberate intervention will necessarily involve replacing existing traditional social norms with specific formal organizational norms. These last two points are critical in the election or selection of cognoscenti ideological constituencies.

The ideological constituencies elected by the cognoscenti are characteristically groups marginalized by traditional social organizations in the larger society: "marginalized" in the sense that traditional social norms govern such persons in these groups differently than they govern other persons. In the early stages of the transformation of the American economy from secondary to tertiary industry and the consequent ascendancy of the cognoscenti the primary focus was upon Blacks, but, more lately, the purview of ideological constituents has been expanded to include LBGTQ-etc. individuals, non-White undocumented immigrants, and others on behalf of whom intervention might be justifiable.

Another critically important ideological constituent of the cognoscenti is organized feminism. While many traditionally oriented women would not describe themselves as feminists, many women, as of this writing in 2023, would. Because women constitute more than half the population, those who support feminism and feminist goals are a huge ideological constituency.

What these groups have in common—and the reason that they were and are elected as ideological constituents for the cognoscenti—is that their integration into the larger society has required, and will continue to require, *deliberate* action—typically, though not exclusively, by government—for *specific* purposes. Such action has disrupted—and will continue to disrupt—traditional social norms prescribing and proscribing behavior and attitudes regarding these groups and their members. Thus, traditional norms are supplanted by the norms of formal organization: deliberately established norms created for specific purposes. The result is, of course, extremely comfortable to people who spend their lives dealing with formal organizations. Even though such government and corporate actions impact their constituencies rather than the cognoscenti themselves, it yields a world cast in the image of the world which the cognoscenti inhabit and which defines them: the formal organization.

The integration of Blacks into mainstream society has required, for instance, a recasting—if only by a restriction of their universality—of familial norms regarding out-of-wedlock births. The application of inclusivity requirements for hiring, promotion, or university admission has required a softening of norms prescribing meritocratic and common standards. Differential levels of criminal behavior have necessitated a re-evaluation of the norms—and sometimes the laws—governing deviant behavior: in all such cases "defining deviance down." In all these instances, traditional norms have been supplanted by norms deliberately established for specific purposes.

And no one individual thinks, consciously, that "Supporting such groups will advance the ideological interests of my own group." Rather, it is that supporting such groups "makes sense" and is "just reasonable" for individuals who live the life of the cognoscenti: support for their constituencies makes the world seem more normal, more tractable, less foreign than it would otherwise be.

Finally, because of the moralization of ideology, it is but a short step from such a position to a position of moral outrage when such intervention into traditional social norms is absent. Such interventions become more than "just reasonable"; they become "only fair" and "morally necessary." Because of the moralization of ideology, violation of these norms becomes not merely a mistake but a breach of faith, a sin, blasphemy, the act of an infidel.

Now, *post festum*, actions to integrate previously excluded (or otherwise disadvantaged or marginalized) groups into the social mainstream using formal organizational arrangements will be accounted for by reference to "values" such as "inclusivity." But such formulations get things exactly backward: the "value" doesn't cause the organizational effort; organizational role (and the parochialism of life experience) causes the value. If "inclusivity," for example, were, in fact, taken to be a transcendent value, it would be generally applied, and there would be no cognoscenti endorsement of such things as all-Black dormitories at universities, no exclusions of Whites from ethnic-studies classes, no support for the National Association of Black _____ [fill in the blank] organizations. No, and we will address this and similar formulations regarding "values" later in this chapter.

Now, it should be clearly understood that such an ideological analysis of cognoscenti ideology says nothing about whether such ideology is wrong or cynical ... indeed, we have said that subscription to the ideology is not deliberate. Our analysis simply and solely endeavors to show the sources of the ideology: in this case, how ideological constituencies are elected for advocacy. The source of an idea has—in a formal logical sense, at least—no bearing on its truth value.

C. THEMES IN THE IDEOLOGY OF THE COGNOSCENTI

1. Why the Cognoscenti Subscribe to Particular Ideological Themes.

The cognoscenti live their occupational lives in rationally established roles working with information, the raw material of rationality itself. Their experience of the social world is an experience largely of orderly and predictable events, events occurring for a considered reason.

One might counter that the cognoscenti spend three-quarters of their time *not* on the job, but almost half of that time is spent asleep, and some of the rest is spent interfacing with other formal organizations. Of the remaining time, most is typically spent with one's family, though declining marriage rates have led to an associated decline in traditional family arrangements ... and some elements of formal organization— e.g., prenuptial agreements—have crept into some marriages.

Beyond this incursion of the formal into the realm of traditional social organizations, American participation in other traditional voluntary associations such as church or synagogue groups, bowling leagues, and fraternal organizations has, as recounted in Robert Putnam's 2000 book *Bowling Alone*, declined sharply since 1950.[30]

---

30. Robert D. Putnam, *Bowling Alone: The Collapse and Revival of American Community* (New York: Simon & Schuster, 2000).

Thus, the social experience of the American cognoscenti has become increasingly the experience of formal organization.

Now, it should be said at this point that the experience of humans in formal organization is not an inherently bad experience: It's all indoors, and there's no heavy lifting … there's no heavy lifting because information has no weight. What is remarkable about such an experience is, though, that it's new. The experience of *Homo sapiens* for the three hundred thousand years of its existence has—except for the past few centuries—been almost solely in traditional social organizations. The statistically normal social setting for human beings has been in small, intimate, slow-changing social groups. The wonder is that humans have proven sufficiently flexible to function in both those traditional groups as well as in modern formal organizations. But to say that humans are flexible is not to say that such a radical change in the experience of everyday human social life is without consequence.

If—on the social level—formal organization has involved deliberately established social organizations created for specific purposes, then what it has brought on the individual—the experiential—level is the subjective experience of social organization and life itself as being deliberately established for specific purposes. This is, historically, a very new normal, indeed.

The ideological themes of the cognoscenti uniformly reflect this novel experience of seeing social life itself as malleable, as something which one—whether oneself or somebody else—creates, tailors, and tweaks to achieve deliberate goals … and a social form which involves life being a deliberately and rationally moldable substance yields a cultural perspective in which life is, naturally, compatible with this social perspective.

The cognoscenti is of historically more recent appearance and must, of necessity, be imperialistic relative to the yeomanry simply in order to elbow its way into a prominent societal position. In addition, the cognoscenti is disproportionately (relative to the yeomanry) based in government agencies and, thus, has some access to the monopoly on (or control of a preponderance of) the means of violence which is—in the Weberian sense—the state's defining characteristic. The cognoscenti is based in organizations which wield power, and the only point in having power is its exercise or the threat thereof.

We have detailed above two sets of factors impacting an individual's likelihood to either produce and transmit or to be receptive to particular ideas. In the first case, such factors as material interest or compatibility with one's experience impact the probability that one will create a particular idea. In the second case, these same factors—*plus* others such as the homogeneity of belief within one's group, the moralization or the fashionability of an idea—influence whether particular ideas are accepted and retained in belief.

David Riesman has provided a model for how characteristic life experiences in the twentieth-century American economy can explain the differences in "social character" between inner-directed manipulators of objects and other-directed shufflers of paper and people. The life experiences of individual members of the cognoscenti are dominated by the characteristics of the organizations employing them. These organizations constitute the "soft" service sector—the part of the economy engaged in the provision of government social services, entertainment, advertising, management, specialized consulting, retail work, and many other services *including those services necessary to maintain the formal organizations themselves.* The work experience in such organizations is not only "socially dense" (i.e., in the sense that one deals with a great many people), it is also "socially manipulative:" one's work involves creating or implementing policies designed to inflect human behavior ... or one creates cultural images of people and their behavior ... or one processes information about people and how they have behaved. Thus, from the psychological perspective developed in the course of such employment, people and their manipulation become the dominating features of one's consciousness of the world. The consciousness characteristic of such experience is, in Riesman's terms, "other-directed." This concentrated manipulation of information is quite an unusual thing in the long course of human experience, an experience which has, for the huge proportion of the population, been a very physical experience, indeed.

This non-physicality—this "social density"—of experience in the services sector produces a consciousness in which people are regarded as manipulable objects and as infinitely moldable. These ideas reflect a particular social base, and this social base itself rests upon a particular mode of economic production. Such ideas involve cognitive beliefs about the nature of people (which are expressed, for instance, in the predisposition to emphasize mutable "nurture" over immutable "nature" in explaining human behavior). Such pronouncements are subsumed by the "human biological exceptionalism" theme characteristic of cognoscenti ideology dealt with below.

Beyond these factors determining the likelihood that an idea will be either created or well-received in a particular social location are those other factors—chiefly homogeneity of common belief, moralization, and fashionability—which determine a group's receptivity to a particular ideology. In the contemporary American context, the operation of these factors is heavily influenced by the electronic mass media. The ideologies promulgated by the mass media are directed not only at the cognoscenti masses but also at the national population at large: that population consisting of the yeomanry, the cognoscenti, the respective constituencies of each sector as well as young, ideologically adrift people, and people in conflicted ideological positions (e. g., occupational cognoscenti in predominantly yeomanry communities).

As is the case with the yeomanry, the cognoscenti will mine traditional bodies of culture and thought for useful ideological materials, and such ideas are particularly valuable because of their legitimacy with the populace. For instance, themes embracing racial equality can be supported by historic ideas about a broader human equality, ideas which antedate the cognoscenti by more than a century. However, such ideas must be adapted to the exigencies of the cognoscenti, foremost among which is the expansion of political power. "Equality," by itself, isn't enough; there must be some implication for the centralization of political power and its application if this is to be a useful theme. A review of the ideological positions of the late civil rights leader, Martin Luther King, Jr., is, in this respect, instructive. During the late 1950s and 1960s, Dr. King advocated an end to racial discrimination, a position which is "passive" in the sense that it sought merely to end onerous practices. Most of the legislative action required in support of such a position had been passed by 1965. A mutually beneficial sponsor/constituent relationship required a more active position, and such measures came to be implemented after Dr. King's assassination. This more active posture involved affirmative action and other policies which required the creation of new and enduring governmental structures for their implementation. This is how "color-blindness" became "racism," compatible with a new—but advantageous—definition of the latter. The idea of "structural racism" (also called "systemic racism" or "institutional racism") comports much more with the idea that society itself needs to be deliberately reorganized with specific purposes in mind than does the conception of racism as a belief or system of beliefs.

2. The Cognoscenti Ideological Themes Themselves.

What follows is not an exhaustive list of ideological themes. Clearly, too, these themes are not mutually exclusive: one can readily see where one theme might "blend" into another, a fact amplified by virtue of the fact that these themes are typically deployed together.

To try to impose some sort of taxonomy on what is a rather lengthy enumeration of ideological themes, we have created a distinction between "primary" themes—which directly reflect the life experience of the cognoscenti in formal organizations and without direct reference to ideological constituencies—and "derivative" themes which derive from the advocacy for ideological constituencies. This distinction has no major theoretical significance, and even the themes so distinguished are not mutually exclusive. That said, the number of derivative ideological themes illustrates the importance of ideological constituencies for the cognoscenti, a condition distinguishing them from the yeomanry.

a. Primary Cognoscenti Ideological Themes.

i. Statism. This theme, involving support for expansion of the power of government in general and the federal government in particular, is the most central in many ideological pronouncements of the cognoscenti. It potentially impacts and amplifies each theme below, and it is asserted in many situations. Statism reflects the experiences of a person who takes their important statuses in life from formal organization. If one's quotidian version of the world is based in formal organization, the clearest mechanism for effecting this formalization of the wider world is the state. And this is true whether or not the individual cognoscente consciously intends that the power of the state be used in this way: from the cognoscenti perspective, the world just makes more sense—feels more familiar—if it is formally organizable, and the natural implementing agency for doing this is the state. Extension and expansion of federal power in particular will be explicit or implicit in most pronouncements of cognoscenti ideologists. Even when local or individual rights are cited as pretexts for action, the defense or protection of such rights will be presented as requiring the exercise or expansion of federal power: whether, for instance, expansion (or contraction) of the First Amendment or contraction of the Second Amendment is being argued, it will almost always be proposed through the mechanism of the state. The exceptions involve expansions of state control over the activities of such cognoscenti affiliates as broadcasters, and even here the truce is an uneasy one. Adherence to the statism theme explains not only the policy positions of the cognoscenti but also the affiliation of this sector with the Democratic Party.

Statism underlies the cognoscenti tendency to style as political topics matters which have hitherto not been conventionally political. Thus—and from the cognoscenti perspective—sex is political; age is political; height is political; appearance is political; obesity is political. This tendency accounts for the cognoscenti proclivity to create neologistic "isms": sexism, heightism, classism, ableism, etc. And this is not cynical: if your life is lived in formal organization, the world makes more sense, becomes more tractable, if everything is political and, hence, falls under the purview of the state. If issues are political, they need a political resolution.

ii. Iconoclasm. Consisting of antipathy directed toward traditional beliefs and norms or toward local or traditional social institutions by the assertion of alternatives or through their derogation, this theme can also be ideologically expressed as an individual's civil liberty to operate outside of the normative structure of these institutions. Examples include the redefinition of the institution of marriage so that it might embrace same-sex couples or the redefinition of femininity to include transgender "women." Historical revisionism—e. g., the reconsideration of the status of the Founding Fathers (particularly those who were slave-owners) and the removal of statues of Confederate generals and Christopher Columbus—also partakes of Iconoclasm. Functionally, the iconoclasm theme serves both sponsors and their constituencies by providing justification for policies destructive of local or traditional social institutions. *Épater la bourgeoisie!* The selection of certain constituency groups by the cognoscenti is both supportive of, and legitimated by, the iconoclasm theme. The advancement of the agendas of, for example, the African American and feminist constituencies illustrate and account for this selection of constituencies.

One can see expressions of the iconoclasm theme in popular culture and, indeed, even in the slang of the nation; consider the use of the adjective "radical" to describe something good … or consider the use of the adjective "bad" to denote something good.

Iconoclasm underlies the cognoscenti view that traditional organizations—families, communities, religious bodies, etc.—are oppressive social forms from which people need and deserve "liberation." Thus, marriage is understood to be an oppressive social arrangement from which women need liberation (notwithstanding that most women do not seek such liberation), or that traditional family arrangements are shackles from which children need liberation (and, thus, that governmental organizations need to intervene on behalf of children to deliver services that have, hitherto, been delivered by families). A recent example of this is the strident public remonstrations displayed in reaction to an editorial published by University of Pennsylvania professor Amy Wax blaming inner-city poverty and other associated problems on the breakdown of bourgeois family institutions and values.[31]

iii. Derogation of Any Localized Locus of Power or Competence.

Whether governmental or private. This is, in some ways, a specific expression of the more generalized statism theme and subsumable thereunder. However, we have chosen to highlight it separately because of its impact on certain anti-constituencies of the cognoscenti. These include, in particular, highly skilled workers in traditional trades such as carpentry, plumbing, automobile repair, and virtually anything else manual which pays well. Such people are frequently presented in the popular culture as being almost thuggish. They aren't thugs, but they are independent blue-collar people (typically male) able to take care of themselves and their families and, on that basis, incompatible with any image of the world which is formally organized. More than simple socioeconomic bias, this denigration of independent competence reflects a view of the world in which legitimate competence and legitimate power derives from one's relationship to formal organization.

This aversion toward local competence is also related to the cognoscenti's discomfort with wealth: wealth is power exercised between organizations or individuals and not power deriving from an office within a formal organization. The farmer, the mechanic, the tradesman, the small businessperson share this "outlaw" character: Their skills and capacity to independently generate wealth give them independence, and independence is something which is looked upon askance by those used to life in a formal organization.

---

31. Jonathan Haidt, *Amy Wax's Defense of Bourgeois Values* (Heterodox Academy: 2017), https://heterodoxacademy.org/blog/in-defense-of-amy-waxs-defense-of-bourgeois-values/

Opposition to private gun ownership and to Second Amendment rights more generally is a specific case of the derogation of localized loci of power or competence theme. Gun ownership is a specific sort of privatized locus of power. In the Weberian conception of the state, the state maintains a monopoly—or, at least, a preponderance—of the means of violence. Private ownership of firearms is ideologically incompatible with this element of cognoscenti ideology.

iv. Rationalism. Formal organizations are deliberately established—and disestablished and altered—for specific purposes. This is to say that they are rationally established. The experience of life in such organizations is the experience of life as rationally ordered. If some complain of the irrationality of bureaucracies, this is simply a rational recognition that some potentially fixable disjuncture exists between the organization's policies and its goals. Accordingly, the cognoscente will tend to look at any situation in a rational way … and this will include topics which the rest of the world looks upon in a non-rational (religious, traditional, emotional) way: marriage, sex, religion, parenthood, honor, etc.

v. Respect for Expertise. This is akin to the rationalism theme. An important subset of it is a respect for science. Closely allied with this is a belief in formal credentials of expertise, credentials issued by formal organizations. One specific expression of this respect for expertise is the cognoscenti's derogation of "stereotyping." Stereotypes are vernacular social science … and the cognoscenti—products of formal organization that they are—have a constitutional aversion to the vernacular. Because of the weakness—relative to the natural and physical sciences—of social science theory, vernacular stereotyping does pretty well by contrast. If you wanted to know where not to park your car in Baltimore, who would you trust more: a social scientist or a cabbie?

vi. Anti-Nationalism/Internationalism. The cognoscenti are suspicious of nationalism. For them the United States is less of a nation—an extended community—than a state. A nation has a national history, a national culture. It is a community—the largest community—in which one lives. A state is a location and its associated population governed by a set of laws and a state apparatus to administer and enforce those laws. Many cognoscenti pronouncements containing this theme verge into "anti-American" statements. Sometimes these are denied; sometimes not.

It is a bit ironic that both "statism" and "anti-nationalism" ideological themes can exist so comfortably together. But here we are ... and, as we have noted, a "state" is different than a "nation."

The cognoscenti regards nationalism as being akin to (perhaps a camouflaged version of) xenophobia—one of the more severe ideological sins of the yeomanry in cognoscenti eyes. The anti-nationalism/internationalism theme also governs the cognoscenti's pro-immigration stance. This positive view of immigration extends beyond the economically useful immigration of highly skilled immigrants to the illegal immigration of low-skilled immigrants from third-world nations whose emigration is propelled by economic or political problems in their home countries and whose acceptance into the US is highly moralized by the cognoscenti.

vii. Secularism. Formal organizations—except for those which are titularly religious—are social environments which make little room for the transcendent. They are deliberately established social entities, established for specific purposes. Life inside of them exposes the individual to little which might be called "divine." As the cognoscenti proportion of the population of the United States has grown larger, the United States itself has, statistically, become more secular.

b. Derivative Cognoscenti Ideological Themes.

i. Redistribution of Wealth. This theme is articulated on behalf of both the constituency groups which would be on the plus side of any such redistribution and on behalf of the agencies which would accomplish it (through higher and more progressive taxes, transfer payments, directed contracts, etc.). The redistribution of wealth theme subsumes not only redistribution *via* the mechanisms of progressive taxation but also through "affirmative action" and other ideological constituency group-preferential policies such as racial "reparations."

Wealth itself is, as we have noted above, ideologically problematic for the cognoscenti. *Inside* formal organizations, power is exercised by the authority of offices within such organizations. Wealth, by contrast, is a medium for exercising power *outside* of organizations: power being exercised between organizations or individuals. From the perspective of the cognoscenti, there is something "outlaw-like" about wealth and about those who possess and use it.

Because of the growing wealth gap between the cognoscenti and the yeomanry, the redistribution of wealth theme bears watching. Redistribution of wealth represents one of the cases in which the "expression of life circumstances" basis for an ideology stands athwart the vested material interest basis for an ideology.

ii. Celebration of the Value of Equality over the Value of Freedom. We will discuss the reverse formulation of this theme in connection with the yeomanry. This theme is articulated on behalf of specific constituency groups whose interests are served by such a prioritization. Moralization is done with reference to the founding documents of the republic and, when the occasion demands, with selected scriptural references. Because people are measurably unequal on almost any dimension on which measurement is possible, equality as a value must be defined by the cognoscenti, for ideologically *moral* purposes, in some way which renders it super-empirical, and—because a social value is a shared value—it must be given a meaning which is both refractory to measurement and shared across large swaths of the society. On the other hand, for ideological *policy* purposes, Equality must be given a measurable definition such that compensatory actions may be taken on behalf of ideological constituencies. In the case of policy implementation Equality will be measured by the equality of outcomes, and policy will be measured in terms of its efficacy in achieving equal outcomes. We will discuss this in greater detail in the last section of this chapter.

iii. Oppression as an Analytical Category. Ideologists of the cognoscenti use "oppression" as a category of thought in a manner which is rather analogous to "the market" in some capitalist ideology. And, in fact, both concepts are more than mere ideological legerdemain. Both come from established bodies of thought of considerable venerability: classical economics in the case of the market, and, in the case of oppression, a tradition that certainly passes through Marx but which is considerably older.[32] Just as capitalist ideologists think in market, cognoscenti ideologists think in oppression; it is one of the reasons such people have such a hard time communicating, why they tend to talk past one another. And, more than talking past one another, people who approach any issues with an "oppression" or a "market" set of analytical

---

32. Those interested in the sources of this tradition are direct to a particularly beautiful and sadly neglected book: Edmund Wilson, *To the Finland Station* (Garden City: Doubleday Anchor, 1940).

categories will automatically cast those issues as being "oppression" or "market" issues irrespective of their category's applicability; if your only tool is a hammer every problem looks like a nail. There is nothing in nature which prevents any concept or category of thought being put to ideological use. Clearly, for cognoscenti ideologists, the oppression theme is a natural resource which can be picked up and used in support of cognoscenti constituencies. The oppression theme is self-moralizing (because, who likes oppression?) and can obviously be used to justify the insertion of law or policy into areas of life which had not hitherto enjoyed such insertion. Oppression is the basis upon which cognoscenti ideological constituency groups are elected to constituency status … and such oppression, moralized, is the basis upon which intervention into traditional social order is ideologically justified. It is interesting, in this connection, to consider the status of Asian Americans in the firmament of cognoscenti ideological constituency groups. Until a recent spate of attacks against Asian Americans associated with the COVID-19 pandemic, cognoscenti ideologists really didn't have much use for Asian Americans; indeed, if anything, Asian Americans were either ignored or treated as a problem because of their self-sufficiency. If oppression is what you're looking for, success and self-sufficiency aren't what you want to find.

iv. Fungible and Transferable Guilt. The idea of the fungibility and transferability of guilt is that guilt, as a "substance," is divisible into small and interchangeable parcels and separable from both the individuals who incurred the guilt as well as from those against whom guilty action was directed … and, thus, capable of being reapportioned among other individuals unconnected with the action which produced the guilt. This theme is articulated on behalf of cognoscenti constituencies and in opposition to anti-constituencies. Its function is to support arguments principally for the redistribution of wealth theme. The function of the assertion of this theme is supporting policies such that, for instance, reparations might be owed by the White population to cognoscenti constituencies irrespective of individual culpability or worthiness.

v. Multiculturalism. Multiculturalism is one of the newer of the ideological themes of the cognoscenti and could also be labeled "inclusivity." It appears in about 1990, though it partakes of the content of older themes such as Fungible Guilt and Oppression. It is asserted on behalf of specific constituency groups and is moralized with references to equality and tolerance. While "multiculturalism" may be used by the ideologues of the cognoscenti, as an ideological trope it doesn't necessarily connote what it sounds like, viz., the equality of all cultures. This is, of course, tied up with the existence, function, and meaning of ideological constituencies. This is how you get from "multiculturalism" to the idea that, within the multicultural firmament, some—specifically, those of the ideological constituency—cultures are better, more worthy, than others. The cultures of one's ideological constituencies are celebrated, and those of one's anti-constituencies (members or constituencies of the other sector) are to be derogated. Thus it is—for the cognoscenti—that White, male, European, "hetero-normative" cultures and their representatives are deplored, and this is true of cognoscenti ideologues who are, themselves, White, male, European heterosexuals. Such is the power of ideology that it trumps one's own self-interest and that of one's own loved ones. This is how the cognoscenti has come to the position that:

- Being Black is "better" than being non-Black … and this, in the context of "anti-racism,"
- Being female or gay is "better" than being male or straight … and this, in the context of "anti-sexism,"

- Being young is "better" than being old … and this, in the context of "anti-ageism."

"Better" in these examples means something like "favorable." Who would you feel more comfortable about disparaging? Who would you rather read a flattering newspaper story about? What would a proper member of your own group prefer?

The reader may have been wondering why the choice of some White and Asian women to wear hoop earrings has been derided as "cultural appropriation" while the choice of some Black women to wear straight hair styles has not. Now you have a theoretical basis—grounded, ultimately, in technological and economic change—to understand why.

vi. Human Biological Exceptionalism. This is the ideological tendency to deny or minimize the significance of the biological differences among populations. Functionally, the theme addresses the interests of several of the cognoscenti's constituencies—which are biologically defined on the bases of age, race, gender, sexual orientation, or condition of physical impairment (e. g., "neurologically diverse")—and also the interests of the civilian agencies and their staffs which have been created to administer policies associated with these groups. Specific pronouncements of the theme will involve the minimization of differences between, for example, men and women or Blacks and non-Blacks. The utility of the theme lies in its implication of the mutability of such differences. ("The differences aren't fundamental or inherent; social oppression created them, so they can be changed by policy.") Such a view of the mutability of racial or socio-sexual arrangements comes naturally to those who live in formal organizations in which all social arrangements are mutable. If such differences in measured performance are not biologically fixed, runs the implicit or explicit argument, then they can be altered, and the natural state of equality regained ("But we have a crying social need for these programs in order to do it."). The current debate regarding the participation of "transgender females" in women's sports is a good example of this ideological theme. One may only wonder what the stunningly rapid development of powerful gene-editing techniques such as CRISPR-Cas9—or DNA synthesis, the capacity to "print" gene sequences—portends for the theme ... not to mention the human condition. Biological nature appears to be much more mutable than any of us had thought. The human biological exceptionalism theme has been a feature of cognoscenti ideology since at least the 1970s when it became rock-solid in the cognoscenti's ideological arsenal.[33] The view which we have maintained is that these themes survive not based on their truth value but on their ability to influence people and policy. There are a few important examples of the expression of the human biological exceptionalism theme, and we shall treat them in detail in chapter XI.

vii. Contemporary Racial Etiquette. In its American sense, racial etiquette refers to how respectable ladies and gentlemen speak of people of a different race. In the American context, this refers mostly to discourse regarding Blacks and Whites. While there is an increasing Asian population in the United States, Asian Americans have been socioeconomically sufficiently successful that they have been declared—at least for certain administrative purposes—"White Adjacent" (and yes, that is a thing).[34]

---

33. Peter Berger captured a bounding example of the theme in the early '70's: "This wing of Women's Liberation .... achieved a certain poetic climax in the statement of a young man about his liberated mate: 'to me she is just a guy with an extra hole.'" Peter Berger, Brigitte Berger and Hansfried Kellner, *The Homeless Mind* (New York: Vintage Books, 1973), p. 199.

34. Kenny Xu, *Critical Race Theory has no Idea What to do with Asian Americans* (Newsweek, 2021), https://www.newsweek.com/critical-race-theory-has-no-idea-what-do-asian-americans-opinion-1608984

"White Privilege"—and, by now, what would have to be called "White/Asian privilege"—refers to the presumption of honesty and competence on the part of Whites and Asians relative to Blacks. For ideological purposes, White/Asian privilege is used as a moral or ethical category in addition to being an analytical category in the sense that there is an implicit or explicit implication that the privilege is unwarranted. Given that the privilege is regarded as being unearned, it is ideologically justifiable to support compensatory actions on behalf of Blacks in university admissions, hiring and promotion decisions and other actions in zero-sum game situations. Indeed, there has come to exist a genre of ideological literature advocating for not thinking of zero-sum game situations in a zero-sum game way.[35] Such actions may be thought of as effecting "inclusion," a morally desirable outcome. It is useful to note, in this connection, that such compensatory actions are independent of (though advantageously compatible with) efforts to achieve "diversity." Diversity—which will be dealt with below—is regarded as being a virtue that benefits all parties.

In the more than four centuries that Blacks and Whites have shared the land that is currently the United States, accepted racial etiquette has peregrinated widely, and one can certainly identify phases in this oscillating cultural process. At one time for a White to have referred to a Black as a "colored person" would have been viewed as proper etiquette (and "etiquette" means "little ethic"); no longer, but "person of color" would currently be viewed as being a phrase which a well-bred White lady or gentleman would use to call a Black person and indicative, of course, of that good breeding. This last point is important: the choice of words connotes more—much more—about the speaker than about the topic of the speech.

---

35. See, for example, Heather McGhee, *The Sum of Us* (New York: One World, 2021).

Negrophilia—or, to put it negatively—anti-racism articulated on behalf of Blacks—is the most salient single item of cognoscenti ideology. It is the most intensely moralized. Its breach will elicit the most powerful response. Negrophilia will manifest itself in essentially every cognoscenti pronouncement about race, the position supportive of Blacks or of blackness/negritude invariably being taken. And racial dimensions will be found in phenomena ("Math is racist!") which one would not have thought to have had a racial dimension. The basis of this is, of course, the radical impact which the inclusion of Blacks in the broader American social order has required and continues to require. As an ideological constituency for the cognoscenti, Blacks have been without parallel.

It is no accident that the Civil Rights Movement surged in the 1960s, coincident with the ascendancy of the cognoscenti. Race slavery had ended one hundred years earlier, but it took the rise of a sector structurally predisposed to an ideology which would be receptive to the civil rights agenda in order to achieve this surge.

viii. Contemporary Sex/Gender Etiquette. Similarly, the terms by which proper ladies and gentlemen (nouns which a cognoscente is very unlikely to use!) refer to one another and the gender-specific behaviors by which they interact with one another have varied over time. The traditional distinction between "Miss" and "Mrs." has largely given way to the ubiquitous "Ms." for the cognoscenti. The former titles denote the familial and marital status of women, and such an acknowledgment of statuses in traditional organizations is unacceptable. In addition, the traditionally chivalrous traditions such as a gentleman holding a door for a lady or of standing when a lady enters a room have largely disappeared among the cognoscenti. The declaration of one's "preferred pronouns" ("he/his," "she/her," "they/their") is, for now, the latest expression of this contemporary sex/gender etiquette theme and reflects a rejection of the traditional view of gender as being biologically binary. These ideological changes are largely due to women having entered not simply the workforce but specifically the cognoscenti workforce: the workforce constituted by the staffers of formal organizations.

The prominence of the "#Me Too" movement in present times has the same source and basis.

There is more than a hint of androgyny in cognoscenti cultural style and ideological fashion. Whether in full-blown "meterosexual" style or in a more generalized softness in the exemplary men and hardness in the exemplary women, the cognoscenti sexual style reflects a world in which work is not sex-typable, a world in which barges are not toted nor bales lifted.

ix. Diversity. We refer here to a propensity to permit—indeed, to mandate—the participation in all spheres of human endeavor by members of identified cognoscenti ideological constituencies. This theme manifests itself in support for affirmative action, including women in military combat roles, allowing transgender people in the military, and so on. Obviously, diversity—as an ideological trope—derives from its compatibility with deliberate intercession in social arrangements ... and that, in turn, derives from the experience of the cognoscenti in formal organization. As we have noted above, "inclusivity" differs a bit from diversity in that the former is morally justified whereas diversity is billed as being a functional organizational good ("getting the advantage of all points of view") in its own right.

D. THE ORGANIZATION OF COGNOSCENTI DERIVATIVE IDEOLOGICAL THEMES AROUND IDEOLOGICAL CONSTITUENCIES

In formulating these themes, cognoscenti ideologists have mined intellectual ore from the historic Left—both the Fabian Left and the Marxist-Leninist Left—as well as having fabricated wholly new thematic material. Statism and iconoclasm may, for instance, be found in both the Fabian and revolutionary traditions as important themes. However, derogation of independent competence and multiculturalism are new themes conditioned by the social exigencies of our time, exigencies which did not exist for the Old Left. Derogation of individual competence is not a flattering theme, and it is sometimes expressed as an image—a literal visual image. It was not ever thus. Visual images of the American worker are parts of the legacies of the WPA (see Plate 1), Thomas Hart Benton (see Plate 2) and the other American Regionalist painters of the 1930s. These were, in their time, associated with the political Left. No more.

PLATE 1. WPA MURAL, COHEN BUILDING, WASHINGTON, D.C.

PLATE 2. LOUISIANA RICE FIELDS: THOMAS HART BENTON

Heroic images from this newer ideological tradition are not of the yeoman farmer nor of the resourceful logger—men who can fix anything with a pair of pliers and a six-inch piece of wire, who can work all night to bring in the crop or make the last load. Heroic images from this more recent ideological tradition are of the single mother who, with the help of food stamps and a kindly social worker, successfully raises her lesbian paraplegic daughter to be the first female Roman Catholic non-believing priest.

The derivative ideological themes listed above are joined, in pronouncements from cognoscenti ideologists, with policy positions specific to its constituencies into three principal clusters:

- The race cluster—the set of positions articulated specifically for the advancement of the interests of African Americans and their advocacy organizations,

- The feminist cluster—the set of positions articulated in support of feminist policies and organizations, e.g., the National Organization for Women,

- The LGBTQ-etc. cluster—the set of positions associated with this self-identified population.

The first thing one notes in this categorization—and in contrast to what we will observe in constituency groups associated with the yeomanry—is that these are describable as "clusters" of policy positions which may be associated with easily identifiable (and already organized) groups. The constituency groups belonging to the yeomanry are much less numerous than those noted above for the cognoscenti and, hence, less "clusterable."

The constituency groups associated with the cognoscenti are all sponsored based on their requirements for federal support or protection and for favorable processing through the media.

The second thing that one notices about this categorization is that—were this being done sixty years ago—there would have been an industrial labor union cluster. However, the ascension of the cognoscenti as a substantial social sector began about sixty years ago such that American union workers—at least from the traditional industrial and trade and craft unions, and by contrast with service unions—are now more allied with the yeomanry and its favored political party, the Republicans.

To digress a bit, this transformation of the American voting public over the course of the last half century is really quite remarkable; such a resorting of partisanship is historically infrequent. In fact, a substantial corpus of political science research has suggested that partisan affiliation is learned early in one's life—is "inherited" from one's parents—and remains very resistant to change over one's lifetime. Green, Palmquist, and Schickler, in their analysis of this matter, conclude that:

> People offer the same descriptions of their partisan attachments over long stretches of time, even when the political context has changed.[36]

36. Donald Green, Bradley Palmquist and Eric Schickler, *Partisan Hearts and Minds: Political Parties and the Social Identities of Voters* (New Haven: Yale University Press, The Yale ISPS Series, nd), p. 39.

However—just as baser carbon can be transformed into a diamond given sufficient time and pressure—masses of American voters have come to change their voting behavior (which is a bit different from party affiliation) and come to support the candidates of parties they once shunned. Thus it is, for example, that the old Democratic "Solid South" of the century-long period between the Civil War and the war in Vietnam came to be transformed into an almost as solidly Republican a region.

Even more prominently than in the case of the yeomanry, the primary ideological themes specific to the cognoscenti and those derivative themes specific to its various constituencies are, by and large, compatible. The various policy positions which are articulated as a part of, for instance, the race cluster—support for affirmative action, contract set-asides, the 8A program itself, special financial support for Historically Black Colleges and Universities, etc.—are generally salutary of other cognoscenti ideological themes: statism and the derogation of local power, multiculturalism, and virtually every one of the others. When constituents' interests collide, there is a reversion to quieter political processes. As of this writing, such reversion is occurring on the issue of public-school vouchers. The use of vouchers produces a collision between the interests of two constituency groups: African American parents, who favor vouchers for the educational options that they provide for their kids, and the teachers' unions, on the other hand, for whom vouchers are anathema because of the erosion which they threaten for their monopoly control of the public-school apparatuses. These are both important constituencies.

As is the case with the yeomanry, the positions taken by cognoscenti ideologists are thoroughly overlain with moralization and defended by reference to principle. Indeed, the cognoscenti is much more intensely potent in this respect—both because large elements of it are state-based and because they are really much better at the ideology business than are the yeomanry. This is, after all, their home turf. The public agencies, universities, advocacy groups, and popular culture producers—an important part of the organizational basis of the cognoscenti—are distinguished by their being culture-producing and culture-transmitting entities. Ideology is a species of culture, and the cognoscenti staff are, in a very real sense, the real professionals in the game. Articulate, well-positioned in their own organizations and in the media, and they themselves convinced, they are their own ideologists in a way that the yeomanry typically are not. The yeomanry must hire people like this to develop and convey their point of view.

As is the case with the yeomanry, the "principles" which are represented as the philosophical basis for ideological statements are themselves one species of that ideology. The principles follow from real material circumstances; they do not lead. This can be seen by the contrasting treatments accorded constituencies and anti-constituencies according to the same "principles." Multiculturalism, to cite an example, is used to defend the use and celebration of group-distinctive cultural features of constituent groups—consider the treatment of "ebonics" as used by African Americans, or the treatment of any sort of "Afrocentric" educational technique. This principle of multiculturalism appears to operate very differently when applied to any use of the Confederate flag or other indicia of southern identity (surely, the anti-constituency "southerners" constitutes a cultural, if not an ethnic, group) or to applying the adjective "Eurocentric" to *anything*.

Indeed, the very different subjective reactions (try it yourself) elicited by the term "Afrocentric" (used as an adjective describing educational techniques, etc.) and "Eurocentric" (used as an epithet) indicate which side is winning this part of the ideological contest. So, too, are the differing visceral subjective reactions elicited by the substitution of "White" for "Black" in front of the various racially distinguished organizations based on occupation or interest (of police officers, history teachers, journalists, Shar Pei owners, etc.). Quite apart from indicating which side is prevailing, such visceral reactions also indicate which side is waging which battle. There are not, for instance, many people out there on the hustings for "Eurocentric" education, and the membership of the National Association for the Advancement of White People seems to be a dreadful bunch of morning-drinking goofballs. Finally, such reactions also indicate the centrality of the mediators of popular culture in forming not only the images appropriate to particular ideological positions but also the acceptability—the fashionability—of even holding such positions.

The case of the now-former state song of the Commonwealth of Virginia may be instructive in this respect. *Carry Me Back to Ol' Virginny* was relegated to the status of being "State Song Emeritus" a few decades back. The leadership in the Virginia state legislature had determined that its lyrics were soft on slavery as well as being written in "Black dialect"— and, thus, racially insensitive—and that such a state of affairs could not be tolerated in the new Old Dominion. So, the old song was retired, and a contest was sponsored to compose a new state song. *Carry Me Back to Ol' Virginny*, it turns out, was written by James Bland, an African American and a former slave, and written … in *ebonics*! Probably the only state song of such provenance and linguistic heritage. However, the unfashionability of the song ("soft on slavery") trumped its authorship by a member of a constituency group, and out it went. We don't just sit around drinking bourbon and branch here in Virginia; we have some real fun down this way.

This matter of the fashionability of ideologies is of enormous importance … however trivial any matter of sheer "fashion" might seem.

121

Fashionability assumes a prominence in proportion with the prominence of the electronic mass media because the producers and transmitters of the popular culture are themselves members of the cognoscenti.[37] The power to define something—some image, person, type of person, idea, clothing style, manner of speech, etc.—as being "fashionable" is a very substantial power indeed. So is the converse, the power to designate something as "unfashionable." The treatment accorded cognoscenti constituencies and their characteristic styles in video broadcast and cable programming is more favorable than that accorded yeomanry constituencies and the yeomanry themselves and their own cultural styles. Cultural themes such as "honor," "fighting words," and "chastity" fare poorly in such an environment, as do the characteristic images of those who embrace them.

It is only through understanding ideology as a matter of fashion that one can adequately explain Tom Wolfe's idea of "radical chic.[38]" The wealthy Manhattan culturati to whom he ascribed this style—both generally and in the context of late '60s and early '70s political styles, their lionization of Blacks—are cognoscenti elites. Their social position both produces certain characteristic ideological styles and puts them in a position to mediate such styles to the general public. Fashion flows, in general, from the upper regions of the socioeconomic structure downward. The fact that lower-status groups may come to be lionized by higher socioeconomic strata is not nearly so well explained (as Wolfe does it) by *Nostalgie de la boue*[39] (a sort of generalized admiration for the lower social orders), and which could—but doesn't—apply equally well to members

37. The exceptions—such as a Rupert Murdock, who is not a supporter of cognoscenti ideologies—seem like anachronisms not long for this world … Antarctic icebergs, as it were, which have drifted too far north.

38. Tom Wolfe, *Radical Chic & Mau-Mauing the Flak* Catchers (New York: Bantam, 1971).

39. *Ibid.* p. 38 *et seq.*

of the yeomanry, as it is by the process of constituency group selection we have described here. In our model, elites and their ideologists from the respective sector select constituency groups based on their compatibility with the ideological requirements of that sector. Fashion is one tool—and a very powerful tool, indeed—in the ideological advancement of the sector's position.

The centrality of fashionability, as presented *via* the mass media, is also illustrated by the succession of acceptable terms referring to Americans of sub-Saharan African descent over the course of the twentieth century. This succession has gone from "colored people" to "Negro" to "Black People" to "Afro-American" to "African American" to "people of color." Fashion changes. The words denote the very same thing, but there has been a succession of socially acceptable usages. To say "colored people" today is the ideological equivalent of wearing baggy olive-drab chinos and white socks: it says more about the characteristics of the utterer than it does about that which is uttered.

E. THE ORGANIZATION OF COGNOSCENTI DERIVATIVE IDEOLOGICAL THEMES INTO SOCIAL THEORETICAL NETWORKS

The creation of social theoretical networks is a phenomenon which significantly distinguishes the cognoscenti treatment of ideology from the yeomanry treatment of ideology. This very substantial difference in how the cognoscenti and the yeomanry organize their respective ideological themes is due, principally, to two social structural causes:

- First, the cognoscenti—by their very nature, literally by definition—process information inside of formal organizations. They are, simply, better theorizers: it's their day job.

- Second, important creators of cognoscenti ideology staff the universities, and, more specifically, the departments of the humanities and social sciences in which networks of all sorts of ideas—including ideologies—are created.

The second point—the prominence of the academy in creating cognoscenti ideology—is particularly important given the predisposition of the twenty-first century university to organize centers of academic practice around areas of perceived oppression (Remember "Thinking in Oppression?"). In actual practice, these centers coincide with the three clusters of derivative ideological themes discussed in the prior section, viz.:

- The race cluster,

- The feminist cluster,

- The LGBTQ-etc. cluster.

This tripartite clustering has both structural and ideological implications.

Structurally—and because formal areas of academic study arise from these clusters—there comes to be a material vested interest and formal academic representation for all of these fields. There exist academic departments of African American Studies, of Women's or Feminist Studies, of LGBTQ-etc. Studies. There are faculty—race profession-als, feminism professionals, LGBTQ-etc. professionals—support staff, journals for the respective fields, national and international conventions and other social arrangements which have economic, career, and political consequences.

Ideologically, such specifically focused fields of endeavor permit the combination and concatenation of the various cognoscenti ideological themes into intricate theoretical constructs detailing the minutia of oppression as they have worked out over the centuries: critical race theory, theories of the history of the patriarchy, theories of nonbinary oppression as a consequence of capitalism, on and on.

And, because we have mentioned critical race theory, a brief digression into critical theory—the more generic antecedent to critical race theory—might be indulged, particularly because the intellectual characteristics of critical theory lend themselves so very well to an ideology based upon the formal organization of the world, a formalization to be achieved by a deliberate intercession in the world. Critical theory—as Max Horkheimer, one of its founders, describes it—must be "normative:" that is, it must take a position on behalf of certain constituencies.

> Critical theory is a social theory oriented toward critiquing and changing society as a whole. It differs from traditional theory, which focuses only on understanding or explaining society...
>
> ... Horkheimer stated that a theory can only be considered a true critical theory if it is explanatory, practical, and normative. The theory must adequately explain the social problems that exist, offer practical solutions for how to respond to them, and abide by the norms of criticism established by the field.
>
> Horkheimer condemned "traditional" theorists for producing works that fail to question power, domination, and the status quo.[40]

Thus it is that social theory of a certain character—that the theory is both normative and its advocates active in implementing those

---

40. Ashley Crossman *"Understanding Critical Theory"* (ThoughtCo, 2019) https://www. thoughtco.com/critical-theory-3026623#:~:text=Further%2C%20Horkheimer%20stated%20 that%20a,criticism%20established%20by%20the%20field.

norms—will have a natural affinity for the ideology of the cognoscenti.

And, of course, because all these ideological corpora are related by their association with the academy, they intertwine with one another and lead to—and how could it have been otherwise?—intersectionality!

Intersectionality involves the interplay—the intersection—of individual orthogonal categories of oppression adduced or identified by these individual bodies of theory such that special "boxes"—hyper-dimensionally defined cells—of oppression are produced by this intersection: hence, the singular character of the oppression experienced by the fat, club-footed Black lesbian. The idea of intersectionality yields boxes of oppression distinct from other apparently similar boxes of oppression by virtue of the unique and uniquely oppressed experiences of people falling into those hyper-dimensionally defined boxes.

Since there are three principal clusters of derivative ideological themes, viz.:

- The race cluster,
- The feminist cluster,
- The LGBTQ-etc. cluster.

one may think of a three-dimensional intersectionality graph—a graphic solid—to describe the axes of oppression in which a hyper-dimensionally-defined cell might exist. Happily, we have not identified additional principal clusters of derivative ideological theme such as one based on age, or geographic location, or so forth; such additional clusters would have required an N-dimensional super-solid of an intersectionality graph.

We are much the richer.

F. "EQUALITY" AS A VALUE

Both "freedom" and "equality" figure prominently in the founding documents of the United States, and both are celebrated as American values in subsequent political literature. Indeed, the themes of equality and freedom figure importantly in the literature of the Western Enlightenment more generally. And there has been a fundamental tension between the two ever since the Enlightenment. As many have noted, freedom and equality do not dwell easily together; they are, in important ways, incompatible. Aside from having two arms, two legs, one head, etc., people are not—in any *measurable* way—equal, differing in size, capabilities, appearance, character and so on. Furthermore, to the extent that these very different people are free to pursue similar goals, they will achieve very unequal outcomes.

Thus it is that—in the contest between freedom and equality—the cognoscenti will generally opt for equality. Equality must be compelled and managed whereas freedom can only be protected, rather than created, by government action. Equality needs to be created because it is not the natural state of affairs ... and that, in itself, is attractive to the cognoscenti.

The cognoscenti will, to be sure, sometimes invoke freedom as a value but only in the breach of its more general fealty to equality. This invocation of freedom occurs most frequently with respect to one cognoscenti constituency or another: e.g., the freedom of LGBTQ-etc. people to "be themselves," or the freedom of Black Lives Matter supporters to protest. But this is only in the breach. Should a baker have the "freedom" to refuse to bake a wedding cake for a same-sex couple because of his or her religious objections to homosexuality ... or simply because of his or her freedom of association ... or must he or she be compelled to bake the cake (or go out of business) in order to achieve "equality" among sexual orientations? For the cognoscenti it's a slam-dunk: Equality ... with a bullet.

The yeomanry will, as we shall explore, do the same thing, but with the prioritization of the values of freedom and equality reversed.

And they'll do it for the same reason. The important thing to understand here is that—whereas individual members of both the cognoscenti and the yeomanry will believe, and honestly believe, that they make their decisions based on their "values"—the truth is that the order is exactly reversed. They derive their "values" from their decisions, and they make their decisions to comport with their own life conditions as well as the attitudes and beliefs of their respective groups (or sectors); further, these sectors are socially structurally—and, ultimately, techno-economically defined. That, in a (somewhat rambling) nutshell, is a sociology of ideology for our time.

VIII. THE IDEOLOGY OF
THE YEOMANRY

IN THE PREVIOUS CHAPTER—DISCUSSING THE sources and nature of cognoscenti ideology—we had an underlying theoretical object—formal organization—to explain that ideology. An historical process struck a population of human beings and turned them into the cognoscenti; this process was the experience of life in formal organization. The ancestors of the cognoscenti were not earlier cognoscenti: they were yeomen. The cognoscenti has, metaphorically speaking, a log-on date.

In looking at the ideology of the yeomanry the key theoretical objects to understanding that ideology are three:

- First, and most obviously, the cognoscenti experience with living in formal organization did *not* happen—not to the same extent—to the yeomanry. The yeomanry—as a social form—had been the statistically "normal" American social type until sometime in the post–World War II period; we have chosen 1960. The American yeomanry was the social form which evolved over the four centuries since initial European colonization of North America up until World War II and which produced the culture which those European Americans—abetted by Native Americans, African Americans, and Asian Americans—developed.

- Second, the yeomanry *reacted* to its displacement (by the cognoscenti) as the "normal" American in ways which impacted their ideology.

- Third—as was true of the cognoscenti—there are contemporary producers of yeomanry ideology.

As the cognoscenti has grown as a proportion of the United States' citizenry over the past sixty years, the yeomanry—once the demographically and socially preeminent sector of that citizenry—has shrunk.

And it shows. For many years, it has been recognized that the social base of fascist movements normally consists of middle-class and working-class people experiencing declining status.[41] The ideology of the yeomanry is in some large part—and to use a very burdened word—reactionary. The adjective "reactionary" carries with it several negative connotations, and we would have preferred that it did not carry such baggage, so let it be said that the yeomanry is reactionary for all of the best reasons. They are reacting to their relative displacement by the cognoscenti.

The term "Coca-colonialization" was used whimsically some decades ago to refer to the displacement of traditional cultural forms by American cultural forms in foreign nations—including nations which are our allies. The yeomanry has experienced something like this with some of the same reaction as, say, the French have had to the incorporation of Americanisms into French speech. An even closer analogy to

41. See, for instance, Seymour Martin Lipset, *Political Man* (Garden City: Doubleday Anchor, 1963), p. 131 *et seq.*

what the American yeomanry have experienced is the social and demographic displacement of Tibetans at the hands of the Han Chinese or the similar displacement of Baltic populations by ethnic Russians. Both the Tibetans and the Balts were and are reactionary in the same sense that the American yeomanry has been.

"Revanchist" and "irredentist" are terms used in discussions of international relations to describe the reaction of a nation or a population within a nation to the loss of territory (revanchism) or to the "loss" of an ethnically similar population occupying that territory (irredentism). In either case, it is a reactionary response to conquest. These terms have been used to describe the reaction of European populations to the loss of territory and population to (and, subsequently, by) Germany during the late nineteenth century and early twentieth century. These terms are appropriate—and that appropriateness is only barely metaphorical—for describing the reaction of the American yeomanry to its loss of hegemony in its own society, its own culture, in the late twentieth century and early twenty-first century. The yeomanry has been displaced as the typical American type, and they long, barely consciously, to get their central place back. Any group–any population recognizing itself to be a group–would.

Second, the American yeomanry live their lives in—and take their principal statuses from—traditional social organizations such as families, communities, religious congregations, local fraternal organizations of all sorts. In previous chapters, we have characterized these traditional organizations as being small, emotionally binding, slow to change, local and parochial, invested with meaning and even myth. Narrow and deep, they produce men and women who take these circumstances to be natural, normal and desirable.

But there is more to the yeomanry ideology than reaction to

displacement and a traditional life experience. That ideology consists of the belief patterns of people who experience life in traditional social organizations, plus the reactionary elements to which we have alluded *plus elements of ideology manufactured by the creators of yeomanry ideology,* and it is to this latter point to which we will next turn our attention.

A. THE CREATORS OF YEOMANRY IDEOLOGY

Whereas academe, Hollywood, the opinion pages of the mainstream media, and other culture-creating institutions loom large in the production of cognoscenti ideology, these sources are substantially absent as producers of yeomanry ideology. In their stead stand what is called, in the common parlance, the "Right Wing Media." This is a blanket term intended to encompass right-leaning radio broadcasts—both local and national—and right-leaning news outlets such as *Fox News* and *One America News.* In the present situation, what sets these media apart from more traditional conservative sources such as *National Affairs, Commentary, The American Conservative,* or even *The National Review* is their enthusiastic and abiding support for former president Donald Trump.

In addition, an important source of "conspiracy theory" misinformation is the combination of anonymous message boards such as *4chan, 8chan, 8kun* and, most famously, *QAnon* which publish misinformation and those people who support such misinformation by subsequently disseminating it *via* the "social media." The authors and purveyors of this misinformation and their motivations are various: some are simply inventing attractive nonsense to make money, e.g., by creating a website and selling ads;[42] some are Russian "troll farms" whose mission it is

---

42. Abby Ohlheiser, *This is How Facebook's Fake-News Writers Make Money* (The Washington Post: 2016), https://www.washingtonpost.com/news/the-intersect/wp/2016/11/18/ this-is-how-the-internets-fake-news-writers-make-money/

to sow discord in foreign nations, including the US;[43] others may be simply entertained to see their own creations—the less plausible the better—repeated.

It must be asked—at least, with respect to the journalists within this group—why they espouse and create ideology for the yeomanry when they themselves are, by social position, cognoscenti: they are—for the most part, at least—college educated professionals working in large, culture-producing organizations. Deviant cases such as this illustrate the limits of the social determination of ideology. Whatever the reason—individual idiosyncrasy, financial remuneration—factors can and do override the social forces at work on individual members of both the cognoscenti and the yeomanry. All of this said, the process of discovery associated with the Dominion Voting Systems libel suit against *Fox News* has disclosed that many of the *Fox News* hosts like Tucker Carlson and Sean Hannity hold private ideas diametrically opposed to those they profess on television. In private they ridicule Trump and his assertions of the Big Lie: that the 2020 presidential election was stolen from him. In private they think more like the theory developed here says such cognoscenti ought to think.

It is ironic that the creation and dissemination of yeomanry ideology has been so profoundly abetted by so new an item of planetary infrastructure as the internet. Indeed, the impact has been qualitative as well as quantitative. Because the social media has made available information unvetted by the norms and procedures of professional journalism, much—perhaps most—of this information mediated to the yeomanry is, in fact, misinformation, i. e., it is demonstrably false ... and those same

43. Scottie Barsotti, *Weaponizing Social Media: Heinz Experts on Troll Farms and Fake News* (Carnegie Mellon University, Heinz College, 2018), https://www.heinz.cmu.edu/media/2018/October/troll-farms-and-fake-news-social-media-weaponization

media make possible worldwide dissemination of that misinformation.

Jonathan Rauch has described the creation of "reality-based" knowledge using the analogy of funnels.[44] In this useful work of applied epistemology, he proposes that the human cultural world is full of assertions, potentially infinite in number, and most of them nonsensical in the sense that—if put through a verification process—they would not be verified. The "funnels" constitute these verification processes, and Rausch cites four (noting that his is not an exhaustive list): scholarship, journalism, government, and law. A more extensive list would include (of course) science, intelligence analysis and forensics of any sort. The epistemological processes vary by domain, but, in general, a select set—the most promising candidates—is chosen from the swarm of assertions and is taken in at the wide end of the funnel, "wire-brushed," tested and vetted by the processes, and a very few come out of the narrow end of the funnel to be regarded as conditionally true: "true" in the sense that they are collectively regarded as describing reality.

Now—and this is critical—there exists, for Rauch, a "reality-based community" of those who have agreed, explicitly and implicitly, that the vetted assertions exiting the narrow end of the funnel are to be treated as being conditionally true: as describing and, indeed, *constituting* reality because all we can know of observable reality is our description of what we observe of it. This is, thus, a rules-based community, and a community is a social object. Because people in this community have subscribed to norms to agree that these assertions, thus vetted, are conditionally true, there can be a shared reality: an agreement about what the world is like, *and this agreement extends beyond the practitioners of the various disciplines involved in vetting assertions to a broader audience which shares these norms, these rules.*

44. Rauch, *Op. cit.*, pp. 95-102, *et seq.*

We have taken this epistemological detour to make the point that some—indeed, a great many—of the sources of yeomanry ideology are not in this reality-based community. They don't subscribe to these norms. They live—intellectually—someplace outside of the reality-based community, that community which exists on the basis of its shared norms—norms grounded in verification processes—about what constitutes truth.

The result of this institutionalized source of misinformation—particularly as amplified by a national leader who himself had and has no great regard for factual accuracy—has been that the yeomanry's ideology has had a very, very substantial adjunct of factual misinformation. Much of what the American yeomanry believes would—in Jean Shepherd's wonderful phrasing—"suffer by over-verification."

B. THE IDEOLOGICAL CONSTITUENCIES OF THE YEOMANRY

The yeomanry does not sponsor a functional equivalent of the ideological constituencies of the cognoscenti. This is, of course, because the central thrust of cognoscenti ideology is to cast the wider world into the form of a formal organization and because constituencies requiring intercession are useful in so casting the world. The yeomanry has no comparably "imperialistic" ideological posture, and, accordingly, no comparable constituencies; by contrast with the cognoscenti, the yeomanry is in a defensive posture.

The ideological constituencies of the yeomanry are those groups which share a role in the *preservation* of the community—most notably, the police and the military—and which espouse traditional values ("duty," "honor," "courage"). While both the police and the military are themselves formally organized, both have cultivated traditions distinguishing them from typical formal organizations, traditions which reflect their roles as *preservers* rather than as *transformers* of their respective communities. Respect for and celebration of these institutions with their traditions of masculinity and righteous violence wielded on behalf of the community puts the yeomanry in sharp contrast with the cognoscenti which has shown ideological expressions extending to outright hostility toward the military and police. This stark difference between the yeomanry and the cognoscenti in their respective ideological perspectives on the military and the police naturally reflects their own life experiences in, respectively, traditional organizations and formal organizations. By their nature, traditional organizations are to be preserved: that's how they get to be traditional. Formal organizations are built deliberately and for a reason ... and they can be, should be, changed for adequate reason. No wonder, then, that one sector celebrates the protection of their traditional organizations and that the other views such protection askance, as an impediment to reasoned and reasonable, morally imperative change.

Such conflict in perspectives between the yeomanry and the cognoscenti leads, obviously, to a conflict between their respective ideological constituencies. This conflict pertains, for purposes of our analysis, not so much to the direct clashes between the constituency groups themselves—e.g., clashes between Blacks and police—as to the clashes between the yeomanry and the cognoscenti and the other sector's constituencies such that the police can become an anti-constituency for the cognoscenti and Blacks an anti-constituency for the yeomanry.

Another—however improbable—ideological constituency of the American yeomanry is the state of Israel, and, by extension, Jews more generally. The remarkable thing about this election of Israel and Jews as ideological constituents is that *it exists, cheek by jowl, with a substantial strain of anti-Semitism in the American yeomanry.* How might such a situation come to be? Anti-Semitism has roots two thousand years deep in Western history, so that its source is not at issue. The real question is how it came to coexist with philo-Semitism. There are a number of candidate explanations, none of which are mutually exclusive. First, the election of Israel and the Jews as a yeomanry constituency may simply be a reaction to the election of Muslims as a constituency by Left-leaning members of the cognoscenti during the twenty-first century and a concurrent sort of Leftist anti-Semitism: another instance of "your anti-constituency is my constituency." Second, the Israelis—particularly in the form of the Israeli Defense Force—have demonstrated themselves to be tough-sons-of-bitches, a term of great approbation among the ranks of the American yeomanry. Third, there is almost certainly some eschatological basis for the philo-Semitism of parts of the American yeomanry. Evangelical Christians make up a disproportionate share of the yeomanry. For many of these Christians, the first adumbrations of the Second Coming of Christ to the Earth are to be marked by a return of the Jews to Zion and a rebuilding of the Second Temple. Now, the end of the world might not be thought of as a cause for celebration by many people, but, for these Evangelical Christians, it is.

Indeed, traditional Judeo-Christian religious groups of all sorts may be thought of as ideological constituencies of the yeomanry. This is relatively new; anti-Catholicism and anti-Semitism have long histories in the United States. In modern times, however, the Evangelical, low-church Protestantism which looms so large in the yeomanry demographic has largely made its peace with Catholicism and (particularly) the conservative forms of Judaism. Islam—due it its embrace by the cognoscenti—is another story altogether.

Finally, the yeomanry will lend their political support to a variety of not-for-profit advocacy organizations which share yeomanry ideological positions: The National Rifle Association, the Daughters of the Confederacy, for example. Such support for ideologically sympathetic organizations is not surprising.

C. YEOMANRY IDEOLOGY AND THE MEDIA

When the yeoman or yeowoman enters into the world of the electronic media, he or she enters into a world created by people unlike himself or herself. The creators and disseminators of information which the media mediates are, by virtue of their organizational lives, cognoscenti. When the yeomanry turns on its television sets and—with increasing frequency—its internet-connected devices, it enters a foreign country with but few friendly consulates. And this is so whether it streams a Hollywood movie, watches a news show, a science show, or a game show; these are all exotica … and, not infrequently, hostile.

Homophily—the tendency to favor and interact with persons similar to oneself—is a universal human inclination.[45] Similarly, confirmation bias—the tendency to seek and interpret information in a way which supports one's own existing beliefs—is a widespread human cognitive characteristic.[46] These two broad human tendencies impact both yeomanry and cognoscenti when they venture into the electronic media, though the two sectors encounter the media under very different circumstances. For the cognoscenti the terrain is familiar, and the natives are people who look, speak and think largely like them. They don't have to look far to find something comfortable.

45. Lars Leszczensky and Sebastian Pink, *What Drives Ethnic Homophily? A Relational Approach on How Ethnic Identification Moderates Preferences for Same-Ethnic Friends* (American Sociological Association, American Sociological Review: 2019), https://journals.sagepub.com/doi/10.1177/0003122419846849

46. Raymond S. Nickerson, *Confirmation Bias: A Ubiquitous Phenomenon in Many Guises* (Review of General Psychology: 1998), https://journals.sagepub.com/doi/10.1037/1089-2680.2.2.175

For the yeomanry the situation is quite different. They must seek out those pockets of yeomanry popular culture—to include the news—with which they might be comfortable. In so doing they fall prey to the purveyors of falsehoods and conspiracy theories that inhabit the right-wing social media and right-leaning, Trump-supportive news media. It must be asked why the yeomanry find themselves so vulnerable to such manifestly falsifiable misinformation. This is a topic, *inter alia,* to which we turn immediately below.

D. IDEOLOGICAL THEMES OF THE YEOMANRY

The following list of yeomanry ideological themes is neither exhaustive nor mutually exclusive. Rather, it is intended to convey the major threads comprising the American yeomanry's ideology and to relate those threads to the social life experiences of the yeomanry, to include both the experience of life in traditional organizations and its reaction to social displacement by the cognoscenti. As we did in the case of cognoscenti ideological themes, we have divided our list into two categories; however, in the case of the yeomanry, our two categories are "politico-economic themes" and "cultural themes." As in the prior case, these two categories do not, in themselves, have any great theoretical utility. Rather, the taxonomy simply clusters things of like kind into a single category, and this arrangement may reduce overlap and duplication. That said, it is striking that the "cultural" themes are more numerous than the "politico-economic" themes; it is no accident that the divide between the yeomanry and cognoscenti has been styled the "Culture Wars."

1. Politico-Economic Themes.

a. Nationalism. The yeomanry is patriotic to the point of jingoism. During and in the aftermath of World War II, Americans were jingoistic … and, let it be said, with some justification. "The Greatest Generation" had gathered from the Depression-era fields, factory floors, small towns and cities and defeated the Axis Powers and Naziism. Not just any nation could have done that. The United States in the World War II era was closer to being a *national community* than, probably, at any time since the founding of the nation and certainly than at any time since. Sugar was rationed; meat was rationed; one couldn't simply buy a new tire. There were "drives" to collect metals and other resources for the war effort. Blacks were not a part of that community, but—of course—they never had been. The sense of a national community resonates well with the rural and small-town experience of the yeomanry, and, hence, the chants of "USA! USA!" come from bleachers filled with yeomen … whether the venue is a sporting event or a Trump rally.

While nationalism might, potentially, find expression along either imperialist and internationalist lines or, by contrast, along isolationist lines, the American yeomanry has chosen the latter, shrinking from foreign wars and international involvements. This is what one might expect from a population based in local communities.

b. Celebration of Property Rights. This theme involves reference to and celebration of the "sanctity" (in the express sense that most rights to property should be privately held) of private property. Defense of the theme is often accompanied by moralized references to natural law and to the experiences of people under socialist and communist regimes. This theme clearly reflects the material interests of those who own *productive* property. It also comes from the experiential basis of living one's life in a situation where property is conventionally owned by individuals or other private entities. The small-town and rural yeomanry will celebrate property rights even when, for example, real estate developers assert such property rights to bulldoze surrounding fields and forests and build suburbs and exurbs to be filled by cognoscenti families. Even beyond government incursion into property rights, residential co-ops, homeowners' associations, automobile leasing—all such institutions which unbundle the "bundle of rights" which constitutes "property"— are unfamiliar to and suspect by the yeomanry.

c. Anti-Statism. This theme describes an opposition to expansion of government power—particularly federal power—*per se*. Anti-Statism can take many forms simply because the range of issues which might potentially involve government expansion is broad. So, one might construe the advocacy of lower taxes, less environmental control, reduced gun control, indeed reduced-any-kind-of-control as species of the generic anti-statism theme. Moralization will include various references to freedom, meddling bureaucrats, and socialism. Wealthy individuals have a variety of reasons to support anti-statist positions, but so, too, do many of the yeomanry; non-Blacks, small-town people—southerners, in particular— have suffered historically a variety of insults from agencies of the federal government and are receptive to the theme. Indeed, the yeoman residents of small, rural states will oppose federal programs even when they are the primary beneficiaries of such programs. The demographically smallest, poorest states are the proportionally largest beneficiaries of federal programs, and they are, in contemporary parlance, "Red," or Republican. The Anti-Statism theme is clearly both reactive against the cognoscenti's Statist ideology and reflective of the yeomanry's small-town and rural experience in traditional organizations.

d. Economic Growth for its Own Sake. Self-explanatory, this is the boomer ideology which is so traditional in American capitalism—in a less charitable view, the ideology of a cancer cell. The images associated with it are of dynamism and prosperity. Moralization often involves references to jobs and to Americanism, however vaguely defined. The theme clearly reflects the material interests of anybody who has an important economic involvement with a business, and, though business owners are more clearly so involved, these material interests are shared, *mutatis mutandis*, by employees, as well. It also reflects life experience in an economically growing world, and many Americans have had such life experiences … and for those who have not had the experience of economic growth, it is a powerful aspiration.

e. A Conflation of Economic and Political Freedom. That there is a relationship between capitalism—or, at least, economic development—and democracy has been known for many years.[47] The fact that an ideological theme is ideological does not make it incorrect. In this particular case, however, expressions of the theme convey that economic freedom—principally the freedom to own and operate a business—is *equivalent to* political freedom, which certainly goes beyond anything a dispassionate observer would claim. The theme is self-moralizing because of the ideological currency of political freedom for all groups—but particularly the yeomanry—in American society.

f. Local Control. Because so many among the yeomanry take their statuses in life from localized institutions—small-town residents, farmers, small business owners, White southerners, for instance—the appeal to local control of social life is a broadly applicable and powerful ideological

---

47. See, for instance, Lipset, *op cit.*, pp. 28, 31, *et seq.*

theme. It reflects both the material interests and the life experiences of people embedded in such institutions. The yeomanry live lives which are localized, and their ideological perspective reflects this reality.

2. Cultural Themes.

a. Individualism. This consists in the assertion of normal civil liberties when they are exercised in a conventional way. So, for instance, the individual freedom to associate—or, in this case, not to associate—with anti-constituencies such as homosexuals or African Americans is asserted, while the individual freedom to, for example, behave in a homosexual manner is not. The sources of this theme are rooted not in material interest but in the experience of life in the uncrowded social ecological settings of small towns and rural areas where the opportunities for social disruption are limited by the fact that, quantitatively, there isn't really much society there to disrupt, and the mechanisms of external social control—particularly the law—may not have a very high profile either. Such small, homogeneous settings do not offer many opportunities to observe unconventional behavior. Such social control as these small-scale settings required comes from the norms internalized by most residents, and these norms prescribe conventional behavior. This is an image of the world cast in a Jeffersonian mold, replete with Jeffersonian ideas about individual liberties and the maintenance of social order. For the yeomanry, social homogeneity—not diversity—is the normal state of things. The social settings in which the human race evolved over the past three hundred thousand years have been small, intimate, and stable communities in which the only bases of social differentiation have been sex and age. "Diversity" wasn't a virtue; to the extent that you had diversity, it might well mean that your community had been conquered and enslaved by that other community from over the hill (or, of course, *vice versa*).

b. A Celebration of the Value of Freedom Over the Value of Equality. Freedom and equality are both prominent values in the founding documents of the United States. They are, as a practical matter, not fully compatible values. In general, the greater the freedom of action permitted people, the more unequal will be the outcomes of such action. Freedom, though easier to measure, can itself be construed in a variety of ways ("freedom from" versus "freedom to," etc.). This fundamental ambiguity of both terms—but particularly of equality—makes it possible to pitch either theme in specific situations. And it's not all a bunch of cynical positioning: either one of the two values might be more applicable in specific situations. However, because of the small-scale private sector backgrounds of much of the yeomanry, the freedom theme is more prevalent than the equality theme, the latter introduced only when material interests are involved, e.g., in reaction to race-preferential policies being asserted on behalf of anti-constituencies of the yeomanry.

It is interesting to consider the naming of small businesses, particularly those engaged in the primary or secondary sectors, businesses which produce things rather than information. One is much more likely to encounter names such as "Freedom Arms," or "Liberty Roofing Supplies" than "Equality Arms," and so on.

It must be said, finally, that there is an important sense in which rural life is freer than urban life. The very human ecology of urban (or even suburban) life, the demographic density of it, means that one cannot do certain things as easily or conveniently as in a rural setting: shoot a rifle, have a bonfire, pee in your side yard. The yeoman or yeowoman is freer in this very physical sense than is his (or her) cognoscente counterpart.

c. Religiosity. This theme—involving appeals and references to traditional religious precepts—might properly be regarded as a species of the local control theme (churches, synagogues, and mosques being important local institutions), but it is sufficiently prominent in its own right that we have segregated it out. The thematic contents are easy to recognize, and the theme expresses the life experiences of people whose intellectual and cultural traditions have remained intact because of being either isolated from or immunized against the forces of the media, urbanism, and secular ideologies. Functionally, the theme operates quite like the local control theme.

d. Opposition to Abortion. The anti-abortion theme is characteristic of certain religious groups (mostly Roman Catholics and low-church Protestants, but including some conservative Jews, as well). It is expressed by yeomanry ideologists in the context of electoral politics and on behalf of those religious groups for whom this is a driving issue. This is an ideological theme with a difference: it reflects nobody's interest (except, arguably, the fetus's interest, and fetuses have neither voting rights nor any other legal status), and it is a bit of a stretch to attribute it to anybody's life experience. Rather, the anti-abortion theme derives from membership in a traditional religious denomination and subscription to a particular reading of Scripture ("Thou shalt not kill."). It is a traditional ideology called forth by the gradual emergence of a medical technology adequate to perform safe abortions, and it is, obviously, reactionary in response to cognoscenti support for abortion.

e. Opposition to Expansions of Gun Control. This is another specific content theme like the anti-abortion theme. The ownership and use of long guns (as distinct from handguns) are largely associated with their recreational use in hunting and target shooting and with a particular social base. Hunting, in particular, is a tradition generally passed down from male parent to male child in American rural and small-town settings. This fact offers an instructive illustration of the changes which have occurred on the American social landscape which is increasingly characterized by female-headed households, urban and suburban ecological settings, and by people immigrating from lands in which private firearms ownership is legally proscribed. These social changes—coupled with appalling local-ized (most prominently urban) problems of handgun and tactical rifle violence in the face of increasingly restrictive legislation—has elicited this theme. It appears in association with the yeomanry because of the sector's rural and small-town character and pattern of residence.

f. Traditional Racial Etiquette. The racial etiquette adopted by the yeomanry is the World War II–vintage American racial etiquette with some changes wrought by exposure to the mass media and changes in race relations which have occurred over the ensuing period. So, the yeoman is likely to say "colored person" (or something harsher) rather than "person of color" and not comprehend the snickering and disdain. Beyond such churlish breaches of ideological fashion, the yeoman is likely to encounter Blacks as being problems or impediments in a way that his grandfather—certainly his great-grandfather—had not. This is true not merely in the case of economic competition—which wouldn't have happened in his grandfather's day—but also in terms of Black street violence going, in the yeoman's eyes, either excused or unpun-ished. Blacks—the single most important ideological constituency of the cognoscenti—constitute an important social problem area for the yeomanry both materially (insofar as they might be impacted by Black criminality) and ideologically, by virtue of what they perceive as the cognoscenti's tolerance for such violence. This is an obvious locus of conflict. The negrophobic style of the yeomanry—very much in contrast to the negrophilic style of the cognoscenti—is regarded as "racist" not only by the cognoscenti but by the wider society as well because of the mediation of cognoscenti ideology to that wider society by the media. And that "wider society" consists of the yeomanry and the cognoscenti together with their respective constituencies as well as younger people who have not been fully imbued with the ideologies appropriate to their ultimate stations in life and people in "conflicted" situations, e. g., a cognoscente who lives in a predominantly yeoman community.

g. Traditional Sex/Gender Etiquette. By contrast with the cognoscenti—whose work life has been powerfully impacted by technologies ending the difference between "men's work" and "women's work"—the yeomanry labor in settings which have undergone relatively little change over the past several decades. The cognoscenti may be relatively uniformly white collar, but the yeomanry is still substantially divided into blue-collar and pink-collar work roles. Accordingly, there has been relatively little change in the etiquette of gender and sex among the ranks of the yeomanry over this period. It is interesting to consider that—even in the industrialized West—men and women seldom encountered one another in the workplace up until the end of World War II. Historically—and prehistorically—men did one kind of work and women did another kind of work and each in a different venue. One would seldom encounter a member of the opposite sex other than a member of one's family—a person covered by the universal incest taboo—except on the Sabbath or some special occasion. Looked at in this way, it is no wonder that the "#MeToo" movement appears only recently. Sex, as a topic, has been the source of humor since time immemorial, and so it remains. It should not be surprising, therefore, that the yeomanry and the cognoscenti taking pot shots at one another over the other side's sex/gender ideological excesses is a frequent venue for skirmish, sometimes taking the form of humor.

h. Virility. Masculinity and the manly virtues—physical courage, honor, chivalry, and the rest—are much more celebrated in the yeomanry ideology than in the cognoscenti ideology. Indeed, one is much more likely to hear reference to "toxic masculinity" in the ideological pronouncements of the cognoscenti than to hear any celebration of male physical courage or honor. To be sure, the work of yeomanry males, in particular, is much more likely to call upon resources such as physical courage than is the work of male cognoscenti. Honor, too, is a necessary virtue in the interactions of small businessmen. Think of deals agreed to on a handshake such as between a farmer and a small-town banker, or a diamond trade done between two Hassidic diamond dealers in New York City. These social arrangements would be impossible without a shared sense of honor.

Finally, the yeomanry are much more likely to have experience as members of the military or police than are the cognoscenti. The ideologies surrounding masculinity are very prominent in these institutions.

i. Nativism. The yeomanry are not only nationalistic they are homophilic: they prefer their own kind. As we have noted earlier, the historic and prehistoric condition of the human race has been to live in small homogeneous communities. The yeomanry—at least relative to the cognoscenti—still do. This is manifested in their skeptical—sometimes hostile—attitude toward immigration. Coupled with their sense of displacement by the cognoscenti, the yeomanry tends to view immigrants not only as economic competition for blue-collar jobs but, even more, as ethnically and culturally alien ... observations which are, to be sure, correct. The predominantly White yeomanry reacts to projections that the US will become predominantly non-White by 2050 in the way that the Tibetans have reacted to demographic displacement by a Han Chinese population or, indeed, the way that Native Americans reacted to demographic displacement by European Whites.

j. Philo-Semitism. Israel—and, by extension Jews and Judaism—constitute one of the yeomanry's ideological constituencies. As we have noted before in this chapter, this philo-Semitism exists in uneasy truce with a powerful strain of anti-Semitism among the yeomanry. We have discussed some of the possible reasons for this philo-Semitism earlier in this chapter: a reaction against newer forms of anti-Semitism on the Left, respect for Israeli toughness, Evangelical eschatology... any and all: we make no mockery of honest *ad hoc-ery*.[48]

k. Anti-Scientism and Disregard for Expertise. This theme refers to a hostility specifically toward the credentialled expertise so celebrated by the cognoscenti. The yeomanry appreciates its own expertise—and it has a lot of expertise—but yeomanry expertise is based in craft and not in science. We have contrasted craft and science earlier in our analysis. The craft of the yeomanry comes principally from the accumulated on-the-job (to include housewifery) experience of generations of craftspeople. It is, in general, not credentialled but rather is popularly recognized by the community. It is a rejection of "book-learning" in favor of more concrete skills. Some of this is clearly reactionary against the cognoscenti. This yeomanry rejection of expertise and of science will become very salient in Section Three.

---

48. We'd love to take credit for this bit of doggerel, but authorship belongs to Robert McGinnis, a former teacher.

These several themes, taken together, would certainly be understood by any informed American of our time as being at least a large component of what we would call "conservatism." They are, however, very different in thematic content from what has passed as "conservative" in earlier epochs. Mannheim, for instance, identifies an "historic conservatism"[49] which he sees to be the residual ideological expression of feudalism, incorporating, as it does, mystical and aristocratic themes. This—and other bodies of ideology which have been called "conservatism"—are very different from the "conservatism" of the contemporary business elite.

An extended discussion of American conservatism is beyond the scope of our current endeavor. That said, Theodore Lowi has, very cogently, made the point that "conservatism" is a term of which, in the context of American politics, far too much is asked.[50] He identifies and distinguishes among:

- Traditional European-style Conservatism—centered on the notion that history has provided us with certain absolute and immutable truths and that these truths and the arrangements based upon them must be conserved,
- Religious Conservatism—centered on the notion that God has provided us with these sorts of truths,
- Business Conservatism or "Nineteenth Century Liberalism," as Lowi calls it—centered on the notion that unfettered human striving in a market economy will produce the best possible world as an outcome (Put this way, it doesn't sound "conservative" at all, does it?).

49. Karl Mannheim, *Ideology and Utopia* (New York: Harcourt, Brace and World, 1936), p. 120 *et seq.*

50. Theodore Lowi, *The End of the Republican Era* (Norman: University of Oklahoma Press, 1995), pp. xii-xiii, 117-121.

And to this might be added, perhaps, "Libertarian Conservatism," though it probably can be subsumed under the last category above. In any event, Lowi points out that these three strains—when contrasted in their specific ideological content—are really *very* different ideologies. A Traditionalist Conservative—as personified, perhaps, by the late William F. Buckley—really doesn't have much in common with, say, the plastic shoe magnate from Bayonne who just wants to be left alone to discharge his carcinogenic effluent into the river. Neither one would wish to bring the other home for dinner to have them meet their families. The Religious Conservatives—which we think of as being more exemplified by Jerry Falwell than by Malcolm Muggeridge—are not very similar to the other two branches either in ideology or in social background.

Now, this is a book about ideology and not about partisan politics, though party affiliation is clearly one expression of ideology. That said, a careful reading of the ideological themes of the yeomanry clearly discloses that the ideology of the yeomanry overlaps only partially with the ideology of American conservatives as it has been expressed historically by leaders of the Republican Party. Republican conservatism has been—in terms of Lowi's triality—"Business Conservatism" coupled with a hawkish national defense posture. The rise of the yeomanry as a self-aware voting bloc presents a considerable problem—as well as an opportunity—for the Republican Party. By contrast with parliamentary systems—in which the legislature selects the executive and in which multiple parties may form coalitions *after* an election—in the American winner-takes-all presidential system interest groups, not parties, need to form a coalition into a party *prior* to elections. Particularly with respect to the "cultural themes" listed above, the yeomanry has only a little in common with the historical Business/National Defense conservatives which had been the dominant coalition constituting the Republican Party.

The Republicans have not, in recent decades, been able to win presidential elections without the yeomanry … but including them is a difficult fit, and the party hasn't yet, as of this writing, figured out how to do it gracefully. A nascent political movement called "National Conservatism" has formed intending to represent the political aspirations of the yeomanry,[51] and new political philosophers such as Patrick Deneen have formulated approaches to accommodating the interests and perspectives of the yeomanry into American political institutions (and, more importantly, *vice versa*).[52] However, the anti-corporate and isolationist inclinations of National Conservatism are hard to adjust with the business and national defense interests which have historically dominated the party. This is a work which—as of this writing—is still in progress, and the challenges are considerable.

E. FREEDOM AS A VALUE

As we saw in the case of the linkage between the cognoscenti and the primacy of equality over freedom as a value, the situation is reversed for the yeomanry. Just as the cognoscenti employs equality as a basis upon which to mold the world into its own parochial image of a proper world, the yeomanry uses freedom as a basis to protect itself from being so molded. We have said that the ideology of the yeomanry is "reactionary" in the sense that it has reacted to the incursions of the cognoscenti into its consciousness and, indeed, into its material spheres of being. The yeomanry responds to such incursions by invoking the value of freedom in support of its position in this situation … not always consciously, but because such a value suits their life situation.

51. *National Conservatism* (National Conservatism, accessed 2022), https://nationalconservatism.org/

52. Patrick Deneen, *Regime Change: Toward a Postliberal Future* (New York: Sentinel, 2023).

We have noted that freedom—by contrast with equality—is a more natural state of things in that it does not require creation and enforcement by sanctions. Equality requires some sort of intervention to make it happen and sanctions to make it endure.

As was the case with the cognoscenti occasionally elevating the value of freedom when it suits an occasional circumstance, the yeomanry will occasionally invoke equality as a value when it involves, for example, an anti-constituency—a cognoscenti constituency—such as Blacks which is also a protected class for purposes of policy decision-making. Thus it is that the yeomanry will support the equal treatment of Blacks and non-Blacks in university admissions or employment hiring or promotion actions.

The important thing to understand is that—whereas individual members of both the cognoscenti and the yeomanry will honestly believe that they make their decisions based on their "values"—the truth is that the matter is exactly reversed. They derive their "values" from their decisions, and they make their decisions to comport with their own parochial circumstances and with the attitudes and beliefs of their respective groups (or sectors); further, these sectors are socially structurally—and, ultimately, techno-economically—defined.

IX. IDEOLOGY, IDENTITY AND FASHION

TO THIS POINT WE HAVE defined and introduced the yeomanry and the cognoscenti, and we have associated them with their characteristic ideological themes by associating these distinctive ideologies with the different life experiences typical to the two sectors. This has been, overall, a sociological explanation inasmuch as most everyday life experiences are social experiences and because the nature of these social experiences differs systematically particularly by virtue of the individual's relationship to formal organization: a bit glibly, whether one experiences that relationship from the inside or from the outside.

A. IDEOLOGY AS A TOTEM

We turn, now, to a different business—a step further in our analysis, utilizing what we have already seen—and we will argue that these ideologies, once created, enter the larger culture as cultural objects in a manner structured by the relationship of the yeomanry and cognoscenti to that larger culture. We shall argue, further, that these ideological cultural objects—along with certain other cultural objects—become totemic objects. A totem is an object which serves as an indicator of one's membership in (or affiliation with) a group. Thus, the totemic object becomes a "badge" of affiliation with that group. Another term—even less metaphorical than "totem"—which might be used to describe this group affiliation function of ideology is "shibboleth." A shibboleth is a cultural custom or usage which serves to distinguish one's affiliation with a group by identifying an out-group. A shibboleth is both inclusionary and exclusionary: it identifies both insiders and outsiders.

The presidential election of 2016 appears to have been a watershed moment in the crystallization of the opposition between the cognoscenti and the yeomanry. The yeomanry—which had voted mostly for Democrats as recently as the 1960s—had been drifting toward the GOP in their partisan affiliations ever since then. In 2016 the American yeomanry voted for the first time as a self-conscious bloc. And they voted, in the race for president, for a man who was overwhelmingly loathed—and with good reason—by the cognoscenti: Donald J. Trump. One is tempted to opine that—if history had been fairer, if it had been kind—the American yeomanry would have been given a nobler champion to lead them: a Fighting Bob LaFollette, a Roosevelt (either one). Instead, they got an amoral, coarse, lying ignoramus: a real estate huckster from Queens. A LaFollette, a Roosevelt would likely not have unified and amplified cognoscenti disdain as did Trump; a nobler leader such as one of these would not have what it took to galvanize the cognoscenti and—in reactionary mode—the yeomanry.

The question may fairly be asked—given the reactive character of the yeomanry's affinity for Trump and Trump's patent unsuitability for the presidency—whether demonstrated executive incompetence or its predictors would have been, in 2016, necessary qualities for cognoscenti rejection of—and yeomanry attraction to—a leader. The answer must surely be "no" inasmuch as the cognoscenti might well reject a potential candidate purely on ideological grounds. Consider the *gedankexperiment* in which a resurrected Robert E. Lee were to offer himself in candidacy for the presidency. Lee—gentlemanly, highly competent both as a general and as an executive, technically educated, well-read, honorable—is the very antithesis of Trump. But surely the cognoscenti would find his traditional, nineteenth-century racial etiquette dispositively disqualifying. A reactive yeomanry would still find him appealing ... and not only because of General Lee's leadership credentials—*and not in spite of them*—but because of the cognoscenti's rejection of him. Trump's manifest unfitness for the presidency was not, in itself, what the yeomanry was looking for, but the united opposition to Trump's candidacy by the cognoscenti was.

We shall return to Trump in a later chapter, but Trump became—and remains, for the time—the single most important totem in the yeomanry's ideological firmament.

That the cognoscenti should reject Trump was overdetermined. Not only does the cognoscenti lean Left ideologically for reasons which we have detailed earlier, the cognoscenti is formed ideologically in the context of formal organization, and expertise is the primary qualification for holding any position in formal organizations. Trump clearly had no credentials of expertise for holding the office of the presidency. He hadn't held public office; he wasn't well-read; he wasn't a good orator ("I have the best words."). He was a multiply bankrupted businessman who had played a successful businessman on television. Trump's lack of qualification was so evident that the most prominent members of the conservative punditry—George Will, Michael Gerson, Jonah Goldberg, Jennifer Rubin, Max Boot, William Kristol, David Brooks, Yuval Levin—all rejected Trump.

This abandonment of Trump by mainline Republicans and Republican intellectuals counted for little within the ranks of the yeomanry. Both major parties had, for many decades, taken the interests of the yeomanry for granted. Yeomanry loyalty had become, by 2016, a loyalty not to party but to people like themselves and unlike the cognoscenti. They voted Republican, but they voted that way because Trump—*much more a mascot than a leader*—had become the unlikely totem of people like themselves.

A devoted Marxist might be expected to view the development of such a "class consciousness" as a good thing:

> No we don't fit in with that white collar crowd;
> We're a little too rowdy and a little too loud;
> There's no place that I'd rather be than right here
> With my red-necks white socks and Blue Ribbon beer
>
> —Johnny Russell

We should expect to hear of multiple documented sightings of Bigfoot before that happens.

The cognoscenti's consciousness of itself, like the yeomanry's, had been building over the course of decades but was brought into sharp relief by the election of 2016. With the foils of Trump and his supporters against which to image and imagine themselves, the cognoscenti, too, recognized themselves as being distinct … distinct, and as being proper people … by contrast with the Deplorables, the yeomanry.

We have spoken earlier of homophily—the tendency of people to seek out and bond with people of their own kind—and both the yeomanry and the cognoscenti have sorted themselves into mostly independent populations. This "Great Sort" has a geographic dimension such that the yeomanry and the cognoscenti generally live in different parts of the nation—and, within the same area—in different neighborhoods.

They work in different occupations, attend different houses of worship, recreate in different hobbies. This crystallization of differences such that the same group of people fall on the same side of *multiple lines of cleavage* is fertile ground for any force of social unrest.

Many commentators have used the adjective "tribal" and its noun form "tribalism" to describe the current political situation in America. We have no compunctions about the use of these terms; we have merely tried to suss out the social organizational dynamics behind the political schism and the technological and economic forces behind the sociology. Jonathan Rauch devotes a full chapter to "The State of Nature: Tribal Truth."[53]

While "yeomanry" and "cognoscenti" are our own nomenclature, the two sectors possess self-identity: i.e., they are aware of themselves as being distinct from and preferrable to the other group. Their own nomenclature for the other group's members is telling. In cognoscenti references to the yeomanry you will hear (besides the aforementioned "deplorables") "rednecks," "goobers," "white trash," "hillbillies," "crackers," "hicks," "racists," "MAGATS," "trailer trash," and other unflattering appellations. The yeomanry's language for the cognoscenti isn't nearly as colorfully varied, and one most frequently hears simply "elites." Most commonly, the two sides use a sort of partisan affiliation shorthand to refer to the other group. Thus, the yeomanry will refer to "Dimocrats," while the cognoscenti will refer to "Trumpublicans" or "GQPers." This has not been the finest hour in our democracy's long political debate.

So, each group is aware of itself as a group, and each group is aware of the other, and members of both the yeomanry and the cognoscenti feel that their own kind are not only the proper kinds of Americans, but they also each feel that their own kind are the proper sorts of human

---

53. Rauch, *op. cit.*, p. 20 *et seq.*

IX. IDEOLOGY, IDENTITY AND FASHION

beings. Once such a pattern of in-group and out-group is established, it sustains itself through in-group loyalty. As Rauch puts it:

> Intergroup animosity need not be about anything, or, at least, not about anything at first. It can be "about" itself: about humans' need to feel part of a group, to defend and protect that group, to show solidarity with friends, and to engage in public displays of animosity toward foes. Once tribal lines have formed, there will be no shortage of ideologies for identity and conflicts to be "about."[54]

With the yeomanry and cognoscenti having coalesced into groups with their own identities and having one another as out-groups, the role of ideology expands to serve a boundary-maintaining function for the respective groups. *This is to say that ideology comes to be a badge or token of affiliation with one's own group and an indicator of non-affiliation with the out-group.* The fact that ideology becomes moralized makes it extraordinarily powerful as a badge of affiliation. The power of ideology in this capacity is on full display in the cases of the yeomanry and cognoscenti. It is particularly striking when in-group ideology militates against personal self-interest ... and wins.

Finally, the fact that ideology becomes a moralized badge of affiliation with a group or "tribe" means that it becomes profoundly difficult for an individual to bring himself or herself to reject such an item of ideology because to reject such an item of totemic ideology is not merely to "change one's mind"; it is to reject one's affiliation with one's group, one's tribe, and such a rejection of one's in-group is one of the most emotionally searing experiences which might occur in a human life. Argument about group-totemic ideological themes is, accordingly, very difficult: if a person adopts an idea not by virtue of reason and evidence

---

54. *Ibid.*, p. 33.

but by virtue of its group-affiliation significance, he or she is unlikely to be persuaded to abandon it by reason and evidence.

We will address the problems elevated by the prior sentence in Chapter XI.

In the case of the yeomanry, consider, for example, the matter of the vaccine against the COVID-19 virus. Opposition to the vaccine itself and to government or corporate mandates that one be vaccinated have become badges of affiliation with the yeomanry. By the summer of 2021 the pandemic had become, literally, a "pandemic of the unvaccinated" with almost all cases resulting in hospitalization or death occurring among the unvaccinated population, itself a minority of the entire population. This anti-vaccine posture among the yeomanry was initiated by Trump's early minimization of the disease, abetted by the yeomanry's distrust of science and scientists, and amplified by the misinformation dispensed by websites and news outlets patronized by the yeomanry. This distorted amplification can absolutely beggar the imagination: that the vaccines are a plot to depopulate the world because they cause infertility, that vaccination introduces a tracking transponder chip … on and on. And this in *a matter of life and death for both oneself and one's loved ones*. Rejecting these highly effective vaccines had become a totem of yeomanry affiliation.

Or—in the case of the cognoscenti—consider the case of race-preferential policies directed at Blacks. The cognoscenti—overwhelmingly White—are constrained by the ideological theme of negrophilia, Contemporary Racial Etiquette impels this sector to support policies which disadvantage themselves and their family members in what are, clearly, zero-sum competitions for desired outcomes. At any one time there are a fixed number of admission opportunities at desirable universities; at any one time there are a fixed number of hiring or promotion opportunities in an employing organization. The more benefits one group gets the less there are for others; this is what defines a zero-sum game. Moreover, to support such policies, the cognoscenti has needed to abandon traditional American beliefs about individuality, meritocracy, and conventional beliefs about "fairness" by virtue of which the better score wins the game. The cognoscenti raises its kids to win but sets ideologically mandated barriers in their way. That cognoscenti kids do well in educational and occupational competitions is a credit to their parents' rearing skills. The barriers are a credit to the power of ideology as a badge of sector affiliation, a totem, a shibboleth.

The foregoing examples are not intended to be cheap shots at the yeomanry nor at the cognoscenti who are all, overwhelmingly, good, solid American citizens; the examples were intended to show that ideology can be sufficiently compelling so as to trump personal (and family) self-interest. Any assertion that "ideology simply reflects material self-interest" is simply incorrect ... except, of course, in the special and very telling sense that maintaining good standing in one's identity group is in one's personal self-interest.

The yeomanry and the cognoscenti aren't stupid; they aren't crazy. They don't have to be. Their ideology does it for them.

B. IDEOLOGY AS FASHION

Now, we have addressed, above, two examples of ideology constituting a badge of group affiliation—one from the yeomanry and one from the cognoscenti—but there are many other such examples characterizing the yeomanry and the cognoscenti. Public expressions of support for any of the ideological themes associated with one's own group are a show of group affiliation, and we have seen how strong the ties of such affiliation can be.

"Fashion" is a noun in the English language generally used to denote items which are exhibited to indicate affiliation with one's favored group. Now, in conventional parlance fashion is most typically used to refer to couture, to millinery: to an individual's choice in dress, in hats, shoes, belts purses, and so forth. And, clearly, such fashion choices are indicative of socioeconomic status and level of sophistication. The same, though, could be said of music: Do you listen to Baroque or country … or classic rock or hip-hop? And the same could be said of one's choices of art, food, and drink (Do you drink buttermilk or kefir, Black Label or Taras Boulba?), personal vehicles, entertainment, and so on.

Socioeconomic status and the sector divide are not the same, even though there is some correlation such that the cognoscenti are, on average, more affluent and educated than the yeomanry. That having been said, the yeomanry/cognoscenti cleavage cuts across the income scale. A self-employed plumber and a museum art director probably have similar incomes, but the former is a yeoman, and the latter is a cognoscente. Moreover, it is likely the plumber and the art director will make systematically different choices in music, in food and drink, in vehicles … and in ideology.

Thus it is that one's ideology comes to be a matter of fashion. One's ideology comes to signal whether one is a member of the yeomanry or the cognoscenti. Just like a belt or a purse, one's ideology indicates one's group affiliation. Beyond this, all the cultural choices that correlate with ideology become indicia of sector affiliation: whether one drives a pickup or a Prius, whether one supports Republicans or Democrats, whether one listens to Country or Hip-Hop, whether one wears work boots or Birkenstocks.

A few years ago it became the fashion among some young rural men to install large, *faux* plastic testicles on the trailer hitches of their pick-up trucks. Quite a sight for the car following. You never saw these "truck nuts," as they were called, on a Prius, a Toyota model which appeared about coincidentally. The cultural clash alone would have forced the poor hybrid off the road.

To call ideology "fashion" might seem to trivialize ideology (and, some would say, fashion as well). *This, however, is a profound misunderstanding of the importance of the linkage between ideology and fashion.* If ideology is fashion—and if fashion consists of the styles embraced by "good" people—then being able to successfully label one's opponent ideologically unfashionable means that you have labeled him or her the opposite of a "good" person, viz., a bad person! This is a profound power, *and a power given its profundity by the concurrence of the ideological community:* All Good People will agree with my position! And the evidence for my opponent's position—and the quality of the reasoning with which it is argued—are irrelevant. How many times has the reader seen, in a debate, one of the parties seek to label their opponent's position "racist" or "sexist" or "socialist," or "elitist" or "communist?"

Her position is racist? His position is socialist? *Quod Erat Demonstratum!* An argument is won by the local popularity of its conclusions or implications and not by the quality of argument or the evidence that supports those conclusions or implications. This is—very literally—argument by popular demand, argument *ad hominem.* The argument is judged not by the evidence for the argument, the strength of its reasoning but by the identity of its proponent. The sociology of ideology which has been presented here accounts for not only the occurrence of such ideological forms but of where and among whom they occur ... and, of course, why.

C. IDEOLOGY, FASHION AND POPULAR CULTURE: THE HEGEMONY OF THE COGNOSCENTI

Now, to say that there are parallel fashion structures which characterize the yeomanry and the cognoscenti is not the same thing as saying that these two fashion structures are equivalent to one another with respect to the wider society … and this is true whether one is speaking of ideological fashion objects or non-ideological fashion objects. The popular culture—not to mention the realm of high fashion—is the province of the cognoscenti. This is what one would anticipate based on our foregoing analysis: the production and distribution facilities for the popular culture are large formal organizations; moreover, the product of these formal organizations is information: culture is learned, shared information.

Thus, what is "fashionable" in the wider society—whether ideologically or non-ideologically—is what is fashionable among the cognoscenti. The cultural idioms of the yeomanry do make occasional forays into the popular culture; for example, Jimmy Carter's southern idiom and his roots in Plains, Georgia, brought a new acceptance of rural southern styles into the popular culture during and for some time after his presidency:

I was country when country wasn't cool.

—Barbara Mandrell, 1981

That didn't last long.

I tried to go to college but I didn't belong
Everything I said was either funny or wrong

They laughed at my boots, laughed at my jeans
Laughed when they gave me amphetamines
Left me alone in a bad part of town
Thirty-six hours to come back down
Am I the last of my kind?
Am I the last of my kind?

Mama says God won't give you too much to bear
That might be true in Arkansas
But I'm a long, long way from there
And that whole world's a lonely and faded picture in my mind
Am I the last of my kind?
Am I the last of my kind?

—Jason Isbell, 2017

So, the popular culture is normally—and for understandable reasons—the culture of the cognoscenti. Indeed, even when the culture of the yeomanry makes a temporary foray into the popular culture, it is because the cognoscenti has gone slumming and picked it up as a fashion for the season.

But we are here not to discuss belts, shoes, and music; we are discussing ideology as fashion. Moreover, because of the moralization of ideology—because ideology conveys individual moral propriety—it is a much more powerful indicator of in-group affiliation than is a belt or purse. So, under the circumstance that the cognoscenti produce, inhabit, and operate the popular culture, cognoscenti ideology is what is taken as being acceptable in the wider society: it is the "received ideology" of American twenty-first century society. As indicia of group affiliation driving a Prius or eating vegan pale in comparison to adopting an anti-Trumpist partisan stance, or supporting reparations for Blacks, or making anti-sexist or anti-homophobic pronouncements. Individual artists are endorsed or "cancelled" (early 2020s vernacular for active shunning) based upon their individual adherence to the received ideology. To be hip in our time is to embrace the shibboleths—ideological and otherwise—of the cognoscenti.

When Rightist commentators make note of this, they call it "virtue signaling," but to so call it at least partially misses the point. Such commentators miss the point that *the received virtues are being signaled to a specific group: the cognoscenti themselves* (and to the much smaller population of the ideologically unattached). The yeomanry are wholly missed by such virtue signaling—indeed, they are often the butt of it ("Hate is Not a Family Value.")—because *the yeomanry is much more an object of the popular culture's received ideology rather than a subject participating in it.*

Because of the moralization of ideology, to be out of fashion ideologically—and compared to wearing last season's dress—means to have committed an abrogation of faith, to have blasphemed, to having been an infidel.

Thus it is that what is fashionable in the popular culture is the fashion of the cognoscenti, and this is so whether one is speaking of style of dress, choice of automobile, manner of speech, choice of cuisine, political party affiliation, or ideology. The societally fashionable choices in all these areas—and others—are cognoscenti choices. Such choices indicate that one has been to the right sort of school, has the right sort of job, and believes the right sort of ideas: the *received* ideology. What is more, such choices are highly moralized, and particularly choices of ideological style: such choices do not present themselves as fashion as it is popularly conceived but as morality—as distinguishing moral people from immoral people.

Now, such choices would obviously not work—would not be

IX. IDEOLOGY, IDENTITY AND FASHION

fashionable—in a homogeneously yeomanry context … but yeomanry contexts are largely absent among the overwhelmingly cognoscenti contexts presented by the media, particularly on television and other audio/video media. That said, yeomanry contexts obviously do exist. Taking the 2020 presidential vote as a rough measure of the relative sizes of the yeomanry and the cognoscenti (and including their respective ideological constituencies)—seventy-four million for Trump, eighty-one million for Biden—the American yeomanry and the cognoscenti are of roughly equal sizes. The yeomanry live out their lives on the job, around kitchen tables, in bars, diners, and deer camps. Such contexts are only infrequently presented in the popular media.

In a deeply important way—and at a profoundly massive scale—the American popular culture does not "look like America."

X. IN THE TIME OF TRUMP

THE TIME OF TRUMP. LET us say, first, that this is, perhaps, an unfortunate locution (though one the former president would likely favor) if only because the United States of America faces a number of profound—potentially existential—challenges which dwarf the 45th president (44th if you consider that Grover Cleveland was both the 22nd and 24th) as problems. These include, *inter alia,* climate change, the meteoric rise of China as a military as well as an economic power, recovery from the COVID-19 pandemic (and preparation for the next such pandemic), a war of aggression by a nuclear-armed Russia against its neighbor, the potential threat of a self-aggrandizing AI and widespread and occasionally violent social unrest. Moreover, Trump is—as of this writing—declining in salience both as a national figure and as a Republican luminary due, in part, to his loss in a civil trial for sexual assault and defamation as well as felony indictments in state and federal courts.

Still, our task in this brief chapter is to address the nexus between the yeomanry and Trump, so we will need to explain why the former president became such an important totem for nearly half of the voting population. It might well be asked why one should even pursue such a goal. After all, the yeomanry and the cognoscenti would exist and be in contention in the culture even had Trump never existed. By way of response, one might offer that for many—at least among the cognoscenti—Trump or "Trumpism" is *the* problem posed by the advent of a politically self-aware yeomanry. And this is not a trivial problem. Charles Murry devotes a section of the final chapter of his most recent book to the topic using the title: "If Whites Adopt Identity Politics, Disaster Follows."[55] We do, as a nation, seem to be well into that process.

We are still in the time of Trump: if that period began in 2016, it did not end in January 2021. Trump's unfounded allegations that he actually won the 2020 election—the "Big Lie"—still resonate with the yeomanry, and Trump, as of this writing, has mounted a presidential campaign for 2024 (a rather remarkable decision for a man who said that the 2020 election was rigged against him). So, the question of this linkage between Trump and the yeomanry is a proper object of consideration.

If one looks to Trump himself—Trump the man—to answer the question of this linkage, one finds precious little explanatory material. Trump's own political philosophy is a *tabula rasa*; he had had a history of voting Democratic and making donations to Democratic candidates … but this is what one would expect from a parvenu aspiring to membership in New York polite society. When exposed to the white-light scrutiny which comes with presidential candidacy, it became clear that "Trumpism" was Trump's own personal brand of solipsism. Nothing in Trumpism exists outside of the skin of Donald J. Trump. Famously unread and narcissistic, Trump was and remains uniquely unsuited to public service at any level. Trumpism is—at least for Trump—essentially

---

55. Charles Murray, *Facing Reality: Two Truths About Race in America*, (New York: Encounter Books, 2021), pp 115-120.

masturbatory: if it makes him feel good, Trump does it or says it.

Now, it must be said that Trump's nationalism, his aversion to expertise, his nativist stances on immigration, and his embrace of traditional racial and gender etiquette resonated with the yeomanry, but one finds none of this in Trump's thinking prior to his presidential run; one finds, as we have said, nothing. He, too, was reactive, sensing what the yeomanry wanted to hear and saying it.

Trump has been described as the world's most notorious liar, but, in fact, Trump is—in Harry Frankfurt's terms—more of a bullshitter than a liar.[56] A liar knows what is true and makes a calculation that the benefits of the lie outweigh the risk of being caught in the lie. A bullshitter like Trump makes no distinction between truth and lie; a bullshitter tries to convey a particular image of himself, saying whatever it takes to do that. He might well tell the truth if it suits a particular situation.

We have argued, in the previous chapter, that Trump's appeal to the yeomanry was principally reactionary: the cognoscenti rejected Trump, so the yeomanry welcomed him. This is well-articulated in the words of conservative blogger, Michael Oberndorf:

> "If you are a liberal who can't stand Trump, and cannot possibly fathom why conservatives would ever vote for him, let me finally fill you in. It's not that we all love Donald Trump so much. It's that we can't stand you. And we will do whatever it takes — even if that means electing a 'rude, obnoxious, unpredictable, narcissist' (your words-not ours) to the office of President of the United States — because what we find more dangerous to this nation than Donald Trump, is you."[57]

---

56. Harry G. Frankfurt, *On Bullshit* (Princeton, N. J.: Princeton University Press, 2005).

57. Michael Oberndorf, *This is About Donald Trump vs. YOU* (RenewAmerica: 2020), https://www.renewamerica.com/columns/oberndorf/201006

The cognoscenti—products of formal organization—recognized his lack of suitability for office immediately: they wouldn't have hired him for a job in their own offices. The cognoscenti—acolytes of expertise that they are—saw clearly Trump's lack of international experience, his amorality, his disinclination to read, his disregard for the norms of executive office and of democracy itself, his authoritarianism as being summarily disqualifying. And this is in addition to Trump's frequent breaches of contemporary racial and gender etiquette. The yeomanry—already alienated from their own society by the burgeoning of the cognoscenti as a component of that society—reactively welcomed Trump.

The reactive nature of Trump's appeal to the yeomanry is key here and key, as well, to understanding several issues, including the emergence of "populist" authoritarian leaders or aspirants in other nations such as Hungary, Austria, Italy, and France. First of all, the fact that the yeomanry was attracted to Trump in large part because of the cognoscenti's rejection of him illustrates the depth of alienation from their own society experienced by the contemporary American yeomanry. The yeomanry—a mere two or three generations ago the American common man and woman, salt of the earth—have become sufficiently estranged from, indeed, despised by, the dominating sector of the society that they would cast their lot with a president like Trump. Many of them must have recognized his deficiencies almost as well as any cognoscente: certainly, they wouldn't want Trump to be their employer; *certainly*, they wouldn't want him to marry their sister. An associated—and equally disturbing observation—is the Trump-supporting yeoman's tolerance for Trump's authoritarian proclivities. It has often been observed that, if a substantial group in a democracy comes to feel that it cannot win at least some elections by democratic means, it will turn to undemocratic means. Such is the alienation of the American yeomanry from the core institutions of American democracy. The fact that political leaders are recruited overwhelmingly from the ranks of the cognoscenti further exacerbates this problem of alienation.

For the moment, at least, support for Trump is the yeomanry's badge of membership in the "Benevolent and Protective Order of Good People." Concomitantly, publicly disparaging Trump is the corresponding badge of membership for the cognoscenti. That our own view is that the cognoscenti have it right on this point is much, much less interesting for our purposes than is the fact that partisan affiliation has become a badge of affiliation not merely with political party but with one's own in-group. The same could be said of manner of speech, style of dress, choice of cuisine, place of residence, and many other cultural choices. And the choices made by the two sectors on all these dimensions—whether ideological or not—are the subject of invidious distinction: one's in-group's choice is deemed to be better by that group's members—better both aesthetically and morally—than the choices made by the other group.

Still, fashion changes, and Trump's salience as a fashion statement will fade with the passage of time ... and, of course, nobody gets out alive. The American yeomanry will, however, abide, and the yeomanry will require—and deserve—political representation appropriate to both their size and their beliefs and character; indeed, such political representation is critical to peace and the public good.

Those readers who—like the author—were doing undergraduate or graduate studies in the late 1960s will recall the call to revolution on campuses of the time:

> Look what's happening out in the streets!
> Got a revolution,
> Got to Revolution!

Hey I'm dancing down the street

Got a revolution

Got to revolution

Ain't it amazing all the people I meet!

Got a revolution

Got to revolution

One generation got old.

One generation got soul.

This generation got no dissertation to hold.

Pick up the cry!

—The Jefferson Airplane, 1969

Well, the revolution finally arrived. Just not the one that the students were calling for. It never is.

The American yeomanry—or at least a substantial part of it—has become radicalized.

The election of 2016 was the end of the 1960s.

SECTION THREE:

TWO REMAINING PROBLEMS

XI. HOW DO WE LIVE TOGETHER?

THE TWO GREAT PRACTICAL QUESTIONS raised by this volume will be addressed in these two final chapters. The first is political—How do we live together?—and will be dealt with in this chapter. The second is epistemological—How can we know what to believe?—and will be dealt with in the following chapter.

As we have seen, the twenty-first century United States is riven by the cleavage between the yeomanry and the cognoscenti. Taking the 2020 presidential national popular vote election results—seventy-four million votes for Trump, eighty-one million votes for Biden—as a rough (and rough because the vote totals include not only the yeomanry and the cognoscenti but others such as their respective ideological constituencies as well) measure of their relative magnitudes, the two sectors of are approximately equal sizes, with, perhaps, a 4 percent edge going to the cognoscenti together with their ideological constituencies.

It is interesting to contrast the relative sizes of the yeomanry and the cognoscenti in our time with the sizes of the contending parties during the American Civil War when unenslaved Southerners constituted only about 18 percent of the national population.[58] Now, we are not yet at war with one another. There has been no declaration of secession. Armies have not been raised. That said, violent clashes have occurred, each side having initiated against the other. Firearms have been used by each side against the other. And on January 6, 2021, the Capitol of The United States was violently stormed by a mob seeking to deter the Vice President of the United States in discharging a constitutionally mandated electoral vote counting process.

The events of January 6, 2021, were—by every objective indication—an attempted coup. Felony charges of Seditious Conspiracy have been brought and proven in criminal court against multiple participants. An attempted coup is a big deal: about the only politically bigger deal would be a successful coup. The American Civil War—itself a big deal—was not an attempted coup. The American Civil War was an unsuccessful attempt, by eleven Southern states, to leave the Union ... similar to the manner in which the British American colonies had initiated a successful attempt to disaffiliate themselves from Britain in 1776 (a mere eighty-five years earlier). The storming of the Capitol on January 6, 2021, was an attempted coup: a happily failed but clearly violent attempt at thwarting the peaceful succession of executive authority. An editorial by three retired US Army general officers in *The Washington Post* advises on the preparations needed in the US military to prevent or respond to a similar insurrection following the 2024 presidential election from becoming a new American Civil War.[59]

58. *North and South in 1861* (Anchor: A North Carolina History Online Resource: accessed 2022), https://www.ncpedia.org/anchor/north-and-south-1861

59. Paul D. Eaton, Antonio M. Taguba and Steven M. Anderson, *3 Retired Generals: The Military Must Prepare Now for a 2024 Insurrection* (The Washington Post: 2021), https://www.washington-post.com/opinions/2021/12/17/eaton-taguba-anderson-generals-military/

A. POLITICS AS AN INSTITUTION

This comparison of the relative sizes of the contesting parties between the American Civil War and the situation in America one hundred sixty years later is intended to underscore the magnitude of the political problem confronting the American political institution, an institution which has not—since the turn of the millennium—distinguished itself by its efficacy. We shall, at this point, take a short but necessary digression into our own view of politics' role in any developed society, any modern nation-state. The role of politics is the *peaceful* adjustment of divergent and incompatible interests and views in a society. This view of politics is morally agnostic save for one single dimension: peace is better than violence; call it an irenic bias. This is a value choice which we have made with which most would agree ... but not all, and there are revolutionaries among the ranks of both the yeomanry and the cognoscenti. On other moral dimensions, though, our conception of the role of the political institution is amoral. The role of the political institution is not to "do good," except, of course in the sense of making peace. The role of the political institution is not to "be fair," though, of course, people's idea of fairness will play into any peaceful adjustment.

We regard human societies to be the product of evolution (powerfully abetted by technology), and evolution does not produce perfection. Sometimes human ontogeny fails, resulting in a physically or mentally imperfect human. Sometimes social institutions fail. Per our view of politics, the American Civil War—or any civil war—represents a failure of politics. War is violent; people die; property is destroyed; grudges remain.

It is, accordingly, our view that both the yeomanry and the cognoscenti are going to need appropriate political representation in our American democracy. Neither sector is going away, and each is of about equal size. It is critical that politics—rather than its alternative—prevail.

So, in our view, words like "politics, "political," or "politician" are not epithets, are not slurs. Quite to the contrary, they describe necessary and admirable features of and roles in human social life in a complex society.

B. CANDIDATE POLITICAL SOLUTIONS FOR OUR PROBLEM

This short digression having been completed, let us now discuss how the divergent and incompatible interests and views of the yeomanry and cognoscenti might be peacefully adjusted.

One very superficially attractive and obvious approach would be for the cognoscenti to simply wait out history: that is, wait for the yeomanry to fade away as a demographic, cultural and political force. This sort of historical withering is what happened to the (primary industry) farm lobby in the first half of the twentieth century and to the (secondary industry) industrial union lobby late in the twentieth century. If one subscribes to this view, history is on the cognoscenti's side, and, certainly, that has been the case for the past two or three generations. The technology which powered the rise of a white-collar cognoscenti is still operating and improving. Why wouldn't it be expected to follow to a natural conclusion with the yeomanry marginalized both demographically and ideologically and leaving a socially and culturally victorious cognoscenti and minimal ideological heterodoxy?

This viewpoint's principal problem is that both the cognoscenti and the yeomanry are—beyond some point—irreducible. The work of tradesmen, craftsmen, farmers, small business owners, factory workers, and those others which make up the ranks of the yeomanry isn't going anywhere for the foreseeable future. Most of what remains of it domestically can't be offshored, and one could argue that most of the automation which can be applied to it has been applied to it. Moreover, the newer technology, and, in particular, AI, which is only now being applied to productive processes, may well cut more into the office work of the cognoscenti than into the work of the yeomanry. To cite a popular bumper sticker: "Everybody Hates Rednecks Until Their Driveway Needs to be Snowplowed."

It is also worth noting in this connection that America's fastest growing ethnic group—Latinos—is, by virtue of occupation in construction, the trades, and small business and attachment to family and church, affiliating increasingly with the yeomanry. So far, this affiliation is more social structural than cultural ... but, as we have seen, culture follows structure. It would—purely for the parochial purposes of our theory— be quite important to see the Latino population ally principally with the American yeomanry. It would be important because such a prediction runs contrary to the conventional political wisdom that Latinos will boost the political fortunes of the American Left.

Whatever the future might bring, right now the yeomanry—together with their ideological constituencies—constitutes something like 47 percent of the population to the cognoscenti's (and their ideological constituencies) 51 percent ... and we've seen that it only takes 18 percent of the population (admittedly, under very different circumstances) to make a civil war in America. Metaphorically, one might regard what is called our "Culture War" as a Civil Cold War, and the Cold War of the late twentieth-century is recalled as being a very frightening time. In any event, in our view the "wait-'em-out" strategy is most imprudent on the part of either sector.

A second strategy for achieving peaceful relations between the yeomanry and the cognoscenti might be to exploit the constitutionally mandated federal structure of our governmental institution. We are, after all, not "America"; we are "The United States of America." That is to say, the states which have been united by the Constitution retain some level of sovereignty based upon that Constitution. Indeed, the term "state" is reserved, in most English parlance, for "nation-state:" fully sovereign entities which are divided into provinces. The thirteen original states of The United States began as British colonies which became states in the conventional parlance in 1783 with the signing of peace accords with Britain and remained in this status until the ratification of the United States Constitution in 1789 at which juncture they become united into the United States of America. Our national flag currently contains fifty stars—one for each state—and that number changes with the admission of new states; the national flag of other nations does not so celebrate their respective provinces. "States' rights" has, of course, been an inflammatory issue from before the American Civil War up to the present, with the yeomanry and the cognoscenti splitting predictably on this issue.

And the states do have different cultures. Despite the homogenizing effects of geographic mobility and the electronic media during the twentieth century, Rhode Island—owing to its Italian Catholic heritage—is different from Minnesota—owing to its Scandinavian and German Lutheran heritage. Massachusetts is a culturally and politically very different state than Mississippi. The persistence of these local cultures owes much to the persistence of local social institutions: families, churches, community organizations, and so on. Whether such local cultural differences are regarded as charming local culture or as deplorable parochialism will depend, of course, upon whether they are regarded from the perspective of the yeomanry or the cognoscenti.

While some sort of exploitation of the American federal system of government is likely going to be one part of a resolution of the conflict between the yeomanry and the cognoscenti—indeed, the states are going to retain some of their unique local cultures no matter what is done—a full acquiescence to a states' rights agenda as it was understood prior to World War II is politically unfeasible. First, it would require a complete concession by the cognoscenti and nothing from the yeomanry ... not to mention that the Blue cognoscenti states might well tire of sending their tax dollars to the Red yeomanry states under such a militantly federalist arrangement. In addition, such an approach would create a situation in which national-level and international-level problems would have a seriously weakened mechanism for address. Any permanent resolution is going to be a product of political negotiation in which there is mutual give and take.

There are, as ever, no quick fixes for big problems.

> For every complex problem there is an answer that is
> clear, simple ... and wrong.
>
> —H. L. Mencken

C. HOPE IN THE LONG RUN: A CULTURE OF SHARED, EVIDENCE-BASED THINKING

So, if the resolution of the conflict between the yeomanry and the cognoscenti is to be a political resolution and not a military or quasi-military resolution, there must be a politically negotiated settlement together with enabling legislation and policy. Our chief contribution toward such a negotiated settlement is to show both parties that their respective deepest beliefs are not transcendent absolutes, that such principles are ideological objects that reflect and are produced by the social circumstances in which they were imagined and communicated. This will, of course, be a bitter pill for many to swallow: that one's morality—one's deeply held ideas about good and evil—might arise from one's social circumstance, that these ideas might not be transcendent, that they might not come from God or Marx or Foucault or Derrida, is to let go of trusted moorings and to drift out on an ocean of possibilities. It's not for sissies.

But discomfort is not a criterion for belief. Education is necessarily discomfiting. There are no "safe spaces," only eddies of self-deceit.

> He who learns must suffer. And even in our sleep, pain that
> cannot forget falls drop by drop upon the heart, and in our
> own despair, against our will, comes wisdom to us by the
> awful grace of God.
>
> —Aeschylus, *Agamemnon*

1. A Shared Reality.

The single most important initiative for mutual tolerance between the yeomanry and the cognoscenti is also the most tedious to achieve; that notwithstanding, we shall propose a few techniques for such achievement. This initiative is the negotiation of a shared conception of reality—at least that portion of reality about which evidence may be collected—on the part of both parties. *Let it be clear that this is not a proposal to somehow "unify" the ideologies of the yeomanry and the cognoscenti* (though a little bit of this will come coincidentally). Their respective ideologies are based in the ways of life of the yeomanry and the cognoscenti; to unify their ideologies would require the unification—the homogenization or equalization—of their ways of life, and this is without the realm of possibility. Rather, our effort is merely to engineer a common way of looking at reality from different perspectives: a method such that perspective-based differences may be mutually understood and, in some cases, bridged.

Moreover, not only will the negotiation of a shared, evidenced-based reality not "unify" the cognoscenti and the yeomanry, it will not end ideological totemism. That is to say, there will still be ideological badges of "membership" in both the cognoscenti and the yeomanry. However, the negotiation of an evidenced-based reality accessible through reason by members of both sectors will force ideological totemism into the realms of the abstract (e.g., "Life is a Fountain." vs. "Like Hell it's a Fountain! Life is a House with Many Rooms!"). Pushing ideological totemism into the realm of the abstract has at least one laudable consequence: pushing totems into the abstract creates greater opportunity for individual yeomen and cognoscenti to escape their socially determined ideological positions and come to conditional accord, by virtue of reason and evidence, on those issues which should be matters of fact.

In an earlier chapter, we have noted that it is difficult to disabuse a person, by reason and evidence, of a position which he or she did not reach by reason and evidence. Beyond this, once such a belief becomes a shibboleth—a totem of group affiliation—then abandoning that belief becomes the act of an infidel, a rejection of that group affiliation itself. This abandonment is very difficult for a member of a social species such as *Homo sapiens*. It may be that the most that can be expected of a shared reality based on reason and evidence is that members of the yeomanry and the cognoscenti come to respect a belief that they do not share because that belief is based on reason and evidence even if refracted by a different perspective. But respect for the other is a lot; mutual respect is key to peaceful co-existence.

Pursuing a negotiated shared reality as a means to achieve a condition of truce between yeomanry and the cognoscenti may seem to be, simultaneously, quixotic, expensive, and dangerously long-term. That said, we do not have the privilege of inaction. Barbara F. Walter, a political scientist who has worked with the US Intelligence Community on predicting insurrections, is persuaded that the US is uncomfortably close to a new civil war.[60] Furthermore, we do not offer any policy suggestions to supplant the long, hard, frequently despised and yet noble slog of conventional American democratic politics. The yeomanry and the cognoscenti are of nearly equal sizes in the American polity with some constitutionally designed overrepresentation of the yeomanry in the Senate and the Electoral College and currently strong representation of the yeomanry at the state and local levels. Their partisan political representatives must find a way of accommodating one another ... and of doing so despite the bitterness and rancor which characterizes contemporary American partisanship. If one substantial sector in a democracy determines that it cannot win at least an adequate number of political battles by democratic means it will likely turn to undemocratic or anti-democratic means.

We agree with Mr. Dooley that "Politics ain't beanbag," but we regard politics as a profession and a worthy one, at that. Skillful professional American politicians working within the framework of American democratic political institutions are going to be necessary to any accommodation of both the yeomanry and the cognoscenti over the coming decades. What we hope to have provided these politicians—those who are currently practicing and those who will follow—is a theoretical framework to help them understand and respond to their respective bases as well as the bases of the other side. The "Culture War" issues of our own time and those which will come to emerge—racial preferences,

---

60. Barbara F. Walter, *How Civil Wars Start: And How to Stop Them* (New York: Crown, 2022).

dealing with non-biological genders, reparations, immigration, all the others and those yet to come—can be accommodated, we believe, by skillful politicians working within the context of American political institutions. But "accommodation" implies a mutual give and take, and this becomes very difficult if the decision-making process is overlain by strata of intensively moralized ideological outrage and disagreement about measurable facts.

The cultural creations of Western civilization are majestic, profound in themselves and in their impacts and numerous. Confronted with the question of naming the finest jewel in that crown of creations many might opt for the music of the Baroque or liberal democracy or one or another form of Western architecture. We regard science—and science broadly understood—as the highest and finest expression of the Western tradition both in the magnitude of its impacts technologically and in its elegance and efficacy as a way of thinking about observable reality. By saying that we are speaking here of science "broadly understood," we refer to the application of a generally scientific way of thought and method to all questions about observable phenomena, i.e., phenomena about which data may be gathered. Thus, we are speaking not only of the work of the recognized scientific disciplines but also of any forensic discipline in which inferences are based upon data under the condition that such inferences can be replicated by independent researchers using other, similar, data similarly collected and measured. By this broader understanding of science we would include such forensic disciplines as intelligence analysis, journalism, scholarship, and criminal investigation. All such disciplines—as well, of course, as the traditional scientific disciplines—make inferences according to a rules-based inferential process shared by members of the disciplinary community. Beyond simple honesty, the most important of these sets of rules involves making inferences based on data, upon measurements of observable phenomena.

Jonathan Rauch, whom we have cited earlier, describes a "reality-based community,"[61] a community of those who provide *or consume* the products of knowledge-creating enterprises. He describes these enterprises with the metaphor of funnels: untested propositions go in the wide end of the funnel, are subject to a rules-based scrutiny process, and what comes out of the narrow end is a sub-set of a few of the original propositions which the *community* concurs to being conditionally true and, indeed, to describe reality: hence, a "reality-based community." Critical here is the fact that this reality-based community consists not only of the producers of such vetted knowledge but of its consumers as well. Very few people have seen the data upon which assertions of the reality of the Holocaust are based. Very few people have seen the data upon which assertions of the reality of climate change are based. This unfamiliarity with the actual data notwithstanding, members of the reality-based community accept such assertions as sound because they accept as legitimate both the vetting processes and the practitioners of the disciplines which do have the methodologies for conducting this vetting, this research: historical scholarship in the case of the first example and climate science in the case of the second.

Now, much has been written about the "separate reality" into which the yeomanry appear to have confined themselves in matters which have become badges of yeomanry affiliation. This includes not only specifically Trumpian issues ("The 2020 Election was Stolen!"), but other issues as well: COVID-19 vaccine acceptance, the plausibility of *QAnon*, and any number of conspiracy theories.

One is put in mind of David Letterman's comment that:

---

61. Rauch, *op. cit.*, pp. 95-96, *et passim.*

America is the only country where a significant proportion of the population believes that professional wrestling is real but the moon landing was faked.

To change not merely the thinking but the *way of thinking* of tens of millions of Americans is, to be sure, a major undertaking, *and it is clearly the case that the yeomanry must yield much more than the cognoscenti in coming to a shared view of what constitutes reality.* That said, the cognoscenti must do some painful review of its own most cherished ideological objects. Let us be clear that our central purpose in this chapter is to find a way for the yeomanry and the cognoscenti to live peacefully together ... and that— pursuant to achieving such a state of comity—we propose that (through mechanisms yet to be discussed) the yeomanry and cognoscenti agree upon some shared reality ... and—pursuant, in turn, to that—the two parties agree that a reality agreed to by virtue of shared, rules-based rational thought applied to shareable evidence constitutes that shared reality. That is why we are doing what we are doing here.

But consider the side benefits! A reality—whether shared or not— which is based upon rational, evidence-based thought is what is taken in our time and circumstance to be a reality based upon good thinking! Good thinking, at least, about ideas for which data may be collected. We have confessed earlier to a bias in favor of peace, preferring it to violence in civil affairs. We must here acknowledge another of our biases: toward rational, evidence-based thought. Now, it might well be observed that biases are easy to divulge when they are widely shared! And this is undeniable, though, as we shall see, even popular biases enjoy more lip service than unwavering subscription.

Another side benefit is the relief which rational, evidence-based thinking brings to the pandemic of disinformation created and amplified by the large social media platforms. The need has never been higher for our citizenry to have the capacity to separate the informational wheat from the misinformative chaff.

2. The Augmentation of STEM in Primary and Secondary Education.

The "good thinking" and "anti-disinformation" side benefits are considerable side benefits, but they are only side benefits: our purpose here is a peaceful resolution (in fact, more of a "truce" than a "resolution") of the conflict between the yeomanry and the cognoscenti. As one might suppose, this is not an initiative which one undertakes and completes one morning. The solutions are all long-term in the sense that they will take decades to implement, let alone to complete. *The process will be harder for the yeomanry* because they will need to disabuse themselves of their ideological proclivity to disregard—indeed, sometimes to despise and reject—expertise in general and science in particular. The most natural place to begin is with public school systems; it must be noted that "systems" is pluralized because there are thousands of local school systems across the land. The easiest—both politically and pedagogically—path forward to cultivating evidence-based thought in the public schools is to augment existing science, technology, engineering, and mathematics (STEM) programs. At the risk of belaboring a previous point, our specific motivation here is not to augment the STEM performance of American K-12 students—though this is, obviously, a side benefit in its own right—but to inculcate more students into the evidenced-based patterns of thought which science requires. Indeed, a part of this effort must be to extend scientific methodology and habits of thought beyond the traditional scientific disciplines and into other areas of inquiry to include social studies and the realm of the social sciences and, to the extent possible, beyond. Any subject lending itself to evidence-based thought should be grist for this mill. It will be helpful to teach in primary or secondary school the application of evidence-based thought to, for example, diagnosing problems with an automobile engine or electric motor or diagnosing a kid's sniffles.

This augmentation of the national K-12 scientific teaching effort will have the additional benefit of blurring the geographic and class differences between the learning of the children of the yeomanry and the cognoscenti. The geographic differences are considerable—both regionally and across the rural/urban divide—and making policy now to enable our grandchildren to communicate across the yeomanry/cognoscenti division is a worthy policy, indeed. And, speaking of policy, the enabling legislation for this policy—as well as the funding—must be federal. States—as well as local governments—will have a role here, but the initiative and the money must necessarily come from Uncle Sugar. One will note that this will come as yet another insult to the anti-statist, tax-cutting ideology of much of the yeomanry.

3. Academe.

Higher education, too, will have a role to play in this effort to move the nation—which consists principally of the yeomanry and the cognoscenti—toward evidence-based thinking. The first task is to examine how the university as an institution has evolved over the past half century ... and the results of that examination are disturbing. The academy—that institution which kept the light of Western higher knowledge burning through the Dark Ages and on into the Renaissance and Enlightenment—has become the bastion of an illiberal Left. Particularly among the coastal universities, and particularly among departments of the humanities and social sciences, there has emerged a received ideology; it is the ideology of the cognoscenti Left, and adherence to it is brutally enforced. Indeed, the university has become something of an ideological finishing school for the progeny of the cognoscenti.

This is unacceptable ... and not only as a matter of the institutional health of the academy but particularly for our purposes, the purpose of fostering evidence-based thought. Free speech is a necessary environment for evidenced-based thought to thrive. As Rauch puts it:

> ... free speech is necessary to make the reality-based community work, and that is why the Constitution of Knowledge (like the US Constitution) so uncompromisingly defends it. But free speech is not sufficient. It provides raw materials in the form of ideas and criticism, but those raw materials are merely the inchoate potential for knowledge until rule-based social checking goes to work.[62]

Now, while this unfortunate state of affairs at the university has taken at least a half a century to evolve, it does, happily, have a relatively quick solution. This solution will, again, require federal regulation and enabling legislation. What is needed is federal legislation to require that any educational institution receiving *any* federal funding—and, critically, the receipt and disposition of federal funding makes these universities *agents of the state*—to undertake both active and passive measures to ensure that the constitutional First Amendment right of Freedom of Speech of students, faculty, and other members of the campus community not be infringed upon nor attenuated. Such legislation and the associated policy can be modeled upon civil rights legislation. After all, Freedom of

---

62. Rauch, *op. cit*, p. 96.

Speech is a First Amendment right and a right upon which *all* other civil rights depend.

The policy associated with the legislation would ensure that there not be designated "safe spaces" for protected speech on campus: the campus itself must be a safe space. Such policy would ensure that faculty not be harassed nor threatened with termination for their expressed views. Such policy would require that visiting speakers not be "canceled" and prevented from speaking *and would require that those parties attempting the cancelling or otherwise abridging free speech be removed from campus by whatever means and for whatever period necessary to ensure these rights.*

Universities would not be literally compelled to ensure First Amendment rights; they might simply forego federal funding: *any federal funding.* Happily, most will go along. To paraphrase a popular aphorism: "Once you get 'em by the [federal funding] their Hearts and Minds will follow."

Now, critics from the cognoscenti Left will cry out on behalf of their ideological constituencies: "This policy will make the university community an unwelcoming and uncomfortable place for marginalized minorities!" And a university does become a community, just as an Army barracks or a neighborhood become communities. Indeed, any situation which constrains a group of people to interact over time will likely give rise to a community.

But being a community is not among the critical roles of the university. The critical roles of the university are three:

- The creation of knowledge—principally through research and scholarship,

- The transmission of knowledge—chiefly through teaching, publication, and lecture,

- The curation of knowledge—traditionally in libraries, though increasingly through the management of archives of digital files.

Now, clearly the first two of these—and the third if one considers book-banning—rely on Freedom of Speech. To the extent that "community" or any other value or virtue comes into conflict with *any* of these three critical roles of the university, that value or virtue must yield to what makes the university a university. Moreover, intellectual discomfort during one's student experience is not an uncommon nor an altogether unwelcome occurrence: changing one's mind in response to new ideas is frequently—perhaps typically—discomfiting. Analogous to the discomfort felt following a vaccination, intellectual discomfort shows that the ideas are working.

But still more could be done in the sphere of higher education, and, again, it would require federal action and funding. We would propose legislation roughly similar to the Morrill Act of 1862, signed into law by then-president Lincoln. This act created the land-grant university system, so called because the federal government granted to each state large tracts of federally owned land to sell in order to fund the creation of a university. Many of America's large, prestigious universities were founded upon the basis of the Morrill Act.[63]

We are not proposing that federal lands be sold to create and fund a new system of STEM universities; some other source of funding will have to be found, and, perhaps, states might be induced to participate in the funding. However, we propose that a system of STEM-oriented universities be created and *sited specifically in yeomanry territory* to bring the benefits of both scientific work and scientific thought into regions where these have not yet sufficiently penetrated. In many—perhaps

---

63. *Land-Grant Institutions: The Morrill Act and Land-Grant Universities* (Montana State University: accessed 2022) https://ag.montana.edu/landgrant.html

most—cases an existing university could be used as a core upon which to build an enhanced STEM structure. The goal would be to create a system—or just a set—of STEM-oriented universities across the land in small towns and cities—think of Virginia Tech in Blacksburg—chiefly in the Heartland and not on the coasts. A host of infrastructure issues—airports, adequate internet bandwidth, and so forth—would have to be addressed during the creation of such a university system.

Such a university system would provide several benefits. In addition to bringing science and scientific thought to the yeomanry and their college-age progeny, it would also augment the STEM human capital of the nation. It would also blur the regional and urban/rural geographic divides currently separating the yeomanry from the cognoscenti. It is a reasonable hope, finally, that these universities would spawn a number of small technology companies—companies which need access to STEM university resources, companies which are often founded by faculty members—in the vicinities of the universities. Such an outcome would be particularly desirable in that it would help to allay the current geographic concentration of the digital technology industry. The larger companies in that industry have concentrated around a few coastal urban areas: Silicon Valley, Boston, Seattle, Washington, DC, and a very few others. Now, some of this concentration is due to many young IT professionals' preference for an urban environment. Such preferences are not, however, universal and perpetual and often change with the advent of marriage and children. Moreover, IT work lends itself particularly well to working from wherever you call home.

Finally, we would propose the creation of several federal scholarships—similar to the Pell Grant system—but focused specifically on STEM majors. We would propose scholarships based solely upon academic qualification and economic need. While these scholarships would not distinguish between the yeomanry and the cognoscenti, the former—as well as other economically disadvantaged groups—might be disproportionally benefited because of their lower level of wealth.

And all of the foregoing is in addition to and not in lieu of the various interventions which have been undertaken by state, local and federal agencies to alleviate the problems of depopulation, opioid addiction and economic stagnation which have plagued the Heartland for the past half century. Now is New. Red is the new Black.

4. The Need to Subject All Ideological Assertions to Evidence-Based Thinking.

In most of the foregoing discussion the burden of change—and change is a burden—has fallen upon the yeomanry. This has been inevitable because all of the enumerated policy changes have been pursuant to expanding a rational, evidence-based way of thinking such that there might be a shared reality about which the yeomanry and cognoscenti might engage in legitimate argument and because the yeomanry have a powerful anti-expertise/anti-science theme in their ideology. The yeomanry have an ideological wound which needs to be healed. The yeomanry are, however, not alone in allowing their ideology to cloud their better thinking.

The cognoscenti ideological theme of human biological exceptionalism is noteworthy in this regard. It is more than a bit ironic that, whereas the cognoscenti deride Evangelical Christians for their rejection of evolution, the cognoscenti support the idea of evolution ... except when it comes to human beings. Moreover, evolution is *the core concept* in modern biology: "creationism" is simply tarted-up religious doctrine. To ignore the role of evolution in the creation of humans is to ignore the tens of thousands of years of separation—and the thousands of generations of reproduction in very different environments—among racial groups,[64] and to ignore that *Homo sapiens* is a gendered species which evolved from gendered primates—themselves evolved from gendered chordates, themselves evolved from gendered invertebrates—is to actively ignore the patently relevant reality of biological gender ... and the genetic basis for gender is buried deep in our phylogeny: it appears hundreds of millions of years before the genetic bases for our being warm-blooded or, indeed, our having skeletons. The cognoscenti's ideological need for human biological exceptionalism is evident: race and gender are biological categories, and to acknowledge that they are products of evolution in humans which distinguish categories of humans is to suggest their immutability. We have examined the bases for human biological exceptionalism in Chapter VII: racial minorities and feminists are important constituencies of the cognoscenti and serve to justify the formal organization of areas of life that had hitherto been traditionally organized.

All ideological themes are moralized; to serve as badges of membership in the in-group—the "good people"—they need to define what good people believe. The intensity level of moralization varies, though, among ideological themes, and—for the cognoscenti—no ideology carries more intense moralization than those ideological tropes associated with human biological exceptionalism. And because the upper ranks of large organizations are populated by the cognoscenti, charges of "racism" or "sexism" can result in career-deflecting personnel decisions. Indeed, punishment may go further than that. National Basketball Association team owner Donald Sterling was forced out of his industry by a charge of racism for remarks made in what he took to be a private

---

64. Reich, *op. cit*, p. 88 *et passim*.

conversation.[65] The noted economist Lawrence Summers was ousted as president of Harvard University for his speculations about the differential representation of men and women in the highest ranks of science ... and not about differences in the *averages* in scientific ability between men and women but about the *standard deviations* of the two distributions.[66] Charles Murray—a researcher cited elsewhere in this chapter—was violently prevented from speaking at Middlebury College, and his hostess was hospitalized with whiplash injury and a concussion inflicted by a violent mob composed of members of that college's community.[67]

So, anti-racism and anti-sexism are the two most aggressively moralized themes in the ideological portfolio of the cognoscenti ... but the differences (and similarities) between different racial groups and the two genders are immanently researchable and measurable and have, in fact, been researched and measured for at least a century. In addition to being researchable and measurable, the differences between the behavior and performance of different racial groups and the two genders are—unlike some phenomena—relatively accessible to the layman. This contrasts with some realities—for example, climate change—which require access to large corpora of abstruse data, specialized equipment and high-level expertise to understand.

One may conduct a *gedankexperiment* by contrasting the thinking of the cognoscenti regarding racial and gender differences with a similar topic which does not have the same ideological loading. Consider for example,

65. Matthew Yglesias, *Donald Sterling's Racist Outburst* (Vox: 2015), https://www.vox.com/2014/4/29/18077046/donald-sterling

66. *What Larry Summers Said—And Didn't Say* (Swarthmore College, Swarthmore College Bulletin: 2009), https://www.swarthmore.edu/bulletin/archive/wp/january-2009_what-larry-summers-said-and-didnt-say.html

67. Allison Stanger, *Understanding the Angry Mob at Middlebury that Gave Me a Concussion* (New York Times: 2017), https://www.nytimes.com/2017/03/13/opinion/understanding-the-angry-mob-that-gave-me-a-concussion.html

the topic of cattle: another social mammalian species. Cattle differ not only between the dairy and beef groups of breeds but—within each group—among the various breeds; they differ by milk production, butterfat production, hardiness, heat-tolerance, on and on. And, certainly, they differ by gender; cows are docile; bulls—dairy bulls, in particular—are large, dangerous animals. Nobody doubts that the differences between cattle breeds are the result of that artificially accelerated evolutionary process called cattle breeding. And nobody doubts that the differences between cows and bulls are due to the biological differences between their respective bovine gender natures, products of the biological evolution of social mammals. One can engage in reasoned, evidence-based conversation about cattle because there is no ideological loading on the topic of cattle. Apply the same approach to humans, and see whether you're invited to the next faculty cocktail party.

This *gedankexpertiment* is particularly important in that the predicted response elicited by it will be that "These people are equating people and cattle!"

No. Just, no.

Moreover, as we have noted, these sorts of human differences are—unlike climate change—verifiable by quotidian human experience. To subscribe, as a layman, to the idea that the climate is changing requires, practically speaking, that one defers to the expertise of climate scientists. The differences between the two genders are tractable by the layman through informed reason.

Early in the twentieth century anthropologists began to create lists of "human universals:" phenomena which have been observed to occur in all known societies. This work was carried forward by Donald Brown and, subsequently, by Steven Pinker, who published, in 2002, a list of these human universals based on a compilation by Brown.[68] Some of these universals obviously relate to gender:

- Male and female and adult and child seen as having different natures,

- Males dominate public/political realm,

- Males engage in more coalitional violence,

- Males more aggressive,

- Males more prone to lethal violence,

- Males more prone to theft,

- Males, on average, travel greater distance over lifetime.

Obviously, the specific cultural expressions of these universal gender differences are going to vary by culture, so these are not "instinctive" differences, but the predispositions are universal.

Even more basic behavioral differences between women and men evidently have a biological—specifically, a genetic—basis. For example, and according to the American Psychological Association (APA), women cry more than men:

> Several factors play a role in an individual's propensity to cry. Gender differences in crying, for example, have been explored for decades and across the world, and all of the studies reached the same conclusion: Women cry more than men.[69]

---

68. Steven Pinker, *Human Universals … Compiled by Donald E. Brown* (first published in *The Blank Slate*, New York: Viking Press: 2002), https://condor.depaul.edu/mfiddler/hyphen/humunivers.htm

69. Lorna Collier, *Why We Cry* (American Psychological Association: 2014), https://www.apa.org/monitor/2014/02/cry

And, of course, almost everybody knows that (though not everybody can say so). It's just that—in this case—we weren't asking everybody. We were asking the APA, and we were asking the APA something which—particularly as it might be extended into emotionality differences between the two genders—is heavily ideologically-loaded.

It goes (almost) without saying that we are talking about distributions here: It is probably the case that the men who cry most cry more than the women who cry least.

When behavioral differences between or among multiple biologically defined groups in a society are observed, conventional sociological or anthropological methodology is to try to replicate the same study in multiple societies—preferably societies with different cultures—to determine whether these differences are based in biology or culture. If the results are the same in multiple cultures (as they are in the examples cited above), then we say that the differences are probably biological in nature. We say "probably" because we are of the persuasion that all science deals in probabilities and not in certainties. Indeed, this is the case with all evidence-based forensic enterprises: you never have access to all the evidence; you don't have evidence, for instance, about that which has not yet occurred. That said, we are proponents of the principle of parsimony: "Occam's Razor." The simplest explanation—the explanation which makes the fewest assumptions—is the best explanation for patterns seen in the data. Lack of evidence is only a part of the problem with conspiracy theories; the other problem is their reliance on multiple (and incredible) assumptions: space-based lasers launched by an international Jewish cabal, pedophile rings operating at the highest levels of national leadership, tracking transponders secreted in vaccines, on and on.

And to mention Occam's Razor brings us to the point of noting that *any evidenced, observable phenomenon is explicable by multiple explanations.* There are multiple ways to account for an observed phenomenon for which legitimate scientific data has been accumulated. In fact, and partially because data collection is so expensive relative to theorizing, any new set of data will find any number of candidate explanations for whatever patterns may be perceptible in these data. In this section, we are discussing the most ideologically charged issues in American political culture. It will come as no surprise, therefore, that ideologically inflected explanations will be in no short supply to account for these ideologically dangerous observations in a way that does the least damage to the ideological themes which underly such ideologically inflected explanations. Occam's Razor is the most useful rule of theoretical thumb in the interpretation of ideologically dangerous data. The simplest explanation—the explanation which requires fewer assumptions—will be the best explanation ... irrespective of its ideological implications.

The foregoing has been to demonstrate that an evidence-based argument *can* be made for a biological basis for sex/gender differences, and this argument appears to run counter to the ideology of the cognoscenti. It is important to note that *we are neither making nor contesting this argument that sex/gender differences are biologically based; indeed, to do so would be inimical to the purposes of this book, one of which is to describe the ideologies of the yeomanry and the cognoscenti without endorsing or condemning either one.* We intend merely to demonstrate that evidence-based arguments *can* be made in this ideologically charged topical area, arguments which run counter to the received ideology.

Similarly, one can make an argument for the origin of differences of behavioral and performance differences in different racial groups in biology rather than in culture or in social practice. As in the case of gender differences, the key variables are all immanently measurable and data have been collected for at least a century in the United States. The variables of greatest interest have been the differences between Blacks and non-Blacks in intelligence as measured by IQ tests and other measures of cognitive aptitude and the differences between Blacks and non-Blacks in levels of violent or criminal behavior. This is due to the use of differences in academic performance and criminality as a justification by non-Blacks for separating themselves residentially, educationally, and socially from Blacks. The differences in these two (in the case of this discussion) dependent variables have been in the same direction whenever they have been measured and have been consistent (with some variation in magnitude) over time. The debate has been over the *causes* of these differences in IQ and criminality. The received view has been largely aligned with the ideology of the cognoscenti: that the differences in both dependent variables are due to socio-cultural causes, viz., racism, however defined, and related forces (the legacy of slavery, etc.). The minority view is more closely compatible with the ideology of the yeomanry: that these differences in IQ and criminality are due to biological differences between Blacks and non-Blacks.

Now, formal data have been collected in this matter. For instance, Charles Murray has recently done a meta-analysis of multiple studies on racial IQ differences. He observes that the magnitude of the differences (as measured by standard deviation) between Blacks and Whites decreased slightly between 1972 and 1987 but has remained constant over the period 1987 to 2019.[70] A summary of results over the past third of a century is a persisting racial difference in intelligence of 0.85 standard deviations, a very substantial difference.[71]

Now, in this more recent analysis, Murray offers much less discussion to the *causes* of the differences between Blacks and Whites on measures

---

70. Murray, *op cit.*, p. 34.

71. *Ibid.*, p, 35.

of cognitive performance than he and his coauthor did in their earlier work *The Bell Curve*.[72] In that earlier work, Herrnstein and Murray clearly suggest that both genetic and environmental causes are at work in accounting for these differences in measured IQ.

Murray has also done a cross-racial analysis of violent and property crime arrests in the United States using data from 13 American cities: those cities which have provided downloadable databases on crime and race. Murray presents his results as ratios of arrests per one hundred thousand population for the two groups. For all violent crime arrests the median of the ratios (of 13 cities) of Black : White arrests is 9.0 : 1, and the mean of the ratios is 9.6 : 1.[73] For arrests for the crime of murder the ratios are even more extreme, with a median of the ratios (of 13 cities) Black : White ratio of 18.1 : 1 and a mean of ratios of 23.7 : 1.[74] Murray provides little in the way of an argument as to why these differences are what they are, but the differences are *massive*: they differ by an order of magnitude and more. Quantitative research in the behavioral sciences almost never yields group differences of this magnitude. Whatever their cause, they could be a reasonable basis for decision-making.

It should be noted that Murray's violent crime data are from thirteen American cities. National data developed by the US Department of Justice (DoJ) are in the same direction as—but are less extreme than—Murray's urban data. Using 2019 data the DoJ has Blacks (about 13 percent of the US population) committing 51 percent of arrests for

---

72. Richard J. Herrnstein and Charles Murray, *The Bell Curve: Intelligence and Class Structure in American Life* (New York: The Free Press, 1994), pp. 269-315.

73. Murray, *2021, op. cit.*, p. 51.

74. *Ibid.*, p. 56.

"Murder and nonnegligent manslaughter."[75] Thus, per the DoJ data, Blacks—about one-eighth of the population—constitute about half of arrests for these crimes of serious violence. One might speculate that the substantial difference in ratios between Blacks and non-Blacks when comparing the Murray data and the DoJ data lies in the fact that the Murray data are solely from urban areas whereas the DoJ data are from all areas of residence in the US. And, of course, the data categories are not identical.

There are, to be sure, multiple explanations—theories—to account for these differences. Looking at the measured IQ differences, these might involve assertions of bias in the IQ tests, racism in their administration, or that the tests might underpredict actual Black performance in subsequent life activities. In anticipatory response to this, Murray cites the results of an APA review of the group difference data, a review which was prompted by Murray's earlier work on *The Bell Curve*.[76] The APA's conclusion—issued without minority dissent—is that none of these potentially confounding factors can account for the measured Black/White differences. Nothing in Murray's 2021 analysis would suggest any change in his earlier argument that genetic differences are at least a part of the reason for these enduring and substantial measured differences between White and Black IQ.

It must be noted that Murray's results for both IQ and violent crime are only for the United States. By contrast with the situation with gender, there is no precisely corresponding cross-cultural data (let alone information regarding human "universals"). Accordingly, one cannot make as strong a data-based argument for a biological as over against a

75. U. S. Department of Justice, Office of Justice Programs, *Statistical Briefing Book* (US Department 0of Justice, accessed 2022). https://www.ojjdp.gov/ojstatbb/crime/ucr. asp?table_in=2&selYrs=2019&rdoGroups=1&rdoData=rp

76. Murray and Herrnstein, *op. cit.*, pp. 43-45.

socio-cultural explanation for these differences in behavior and performance by race.

Given the importance accorded the legacy of race slavery in the United States by the cognoscenti Left, it would be important to see if Murray's results would be replicated in societies with no history of race slavery such as some in Sub-Saharan Africa or some European nations, societies which have significant Caucasian or Asian populations with which Black performance might be compared. If the results could *not* be replicated in such a society, it would give much greater credibility to socio-cultural explanations of these performance and behavioral differences. If the results were to be replicated in spite of the absence of a history of slavery then the biological explanation becomes much more persuasive.

One could certainly make evidence-based rational arguments for other ideologically fraught topics which lie outside of the thematic area of human biological exceptionalism. In these areas, too, we would be looking for the cognoscenti and the yeomanry to entertain arguments from the other side based on their scientific merits rather than upon their ideological impact. A couple of examples:

- There is some basis in the literature to think that "diversity" in a society comes with some substantial costs. For example, Robert Putnam has found that ethnic diversity is associated with erosion of what he (following Alexis de *Tocqueville*) calls "social capital." People's levels of trust—including trust in people of their *own* ethnicity—decline under conditions of diversity.[77]

- One might reasonably argue that it is much easier to explain

---

77. Robert D. Putnam, *E Pluribus Unum: Diversity and Community in the Twenty-First Century: The 2006 Johan Skytte Prize Lecture* (Wiley Online Library: 2007), https://onlinelibrary.wiley.com/doi/abs/10.1111/j.1467-9477.2007.00176.x

transgenderism—or "gender dysphoria"—on the basis of delusion rather than using some sort of gender-essentialist explanation. After all, delusion is a defined condition. This is a special case of Occam's Razor in that using a defined condition is arguably a more parsimonious explanation than inventing a new one. And there is no implication that the transgender person is dissembling; they're just wrong, and this mistake persists for more than thirty days; that makes it delusional. Moreover, and ironically, "gender-essentialism"—the idea that a person is "essentially male" or "essentially female"—is, as an ideological trope, much more compatible with conservative ideology than it is with progressive ideology.

As was the case with gender behavioral differences, *our purpose here is not to argue for a biological basis for behavioral differences among racial groups—nor to counter such arguments*—but to demonstrate that data supporting rational, data-based arguments for biological differences in this ideologically laden space are abundantly available. Indeed, it would be corrosive of the purposes of this book to take a stand either for or against the respective arguments. And the reason for such even-handed restraint is that the best way to foster civil discourse across the yeomanry/cognoscenti divide is to move both groups toward a rational, data-based way of thinking about any subject—any subject—about which data may be collected. The yeomanry have further to move in this respect, but it's not enough for the cognoscenti to remain stationary. Civil discourse, not to mention intellectual honesty, demands that the rules of accepted thinking constrain all parties in the same way.

5. Isn't This Just Too Dangerous to Think About?

But wouldn't it be better, one might ask, if—considering the fraught history of race and gender in (at least) our society—we not examine these topics in the same way that we examine others? Wouldn't it be better for our society to live with our myths—if they are myths—for the sake of social peace? Our answer is, of course, a resounding "no." Once one commits to rational, evidence-based thinking about those topics for which evidence may be collected—and that is what we are arguing for here—there can be no exceptions, or the terms of the negotiated social contract will have been breached. And there are no exceptions—for us, at least—because we are asserting such evidence-based thought as an avenue to social peace itself, and an avenue to social peace requires the sort of legitimacy that only comes from even-handedness and intellectual honesty.

We understand that we are making a big and a consequential assertion: We are saying that ideas about which evidence may be found—data collected and analyzed—ought to be subject to reasoned analysis and ought not be left in the realm of faith and ideology. Those who rejected the ideas of Galileo and Darwin on the basis of faith historically came a cropper. Faith—whether it is in the ideology of one's group or in some higher power—has no place in the consideration of matters about which data can be collected.

In a reasoned, evidence-based discussion there is no room for arguments *ad hominem*. In a reasoned, evidence-based discussion there are no bad people, only bad arguments.

Not all would agree. David Reich—Professor of Genetics at Harvard Medical School and a Howard Hughes Medical Institute

Investigator—describes in some detail a very different view expressed by a political scientist. She (the political scientist) proposed:

> ... that research and even emails discussing biological differences across populations should be banned, and that the United States "should issue a regulation prohibiting its staff or grantees ... from publishing in any form—including internal documents and citations to other studies—claims about genetics associated with variables of race, ethnicity, nationality, or any other category of population that is observed as heritable unless statistically significant disparities between groups exist and description of these will yield clear benefits for public health, as deemed by a standing committee to which these claims must be submitted and authorized."[78]

Reich, to his credit, acknowledges the problems which might be posed by his studies of ancient DNA:

> So how should we prepare for the likelihood that, in the coming years, genetic studies will show that behavioral or cognitive traits are influenced by genetic variation, and that these traits will differ on average across human populations, both with regard to their average and their variation within populations?[79]

And—again, to his credit—he comes up with an answer essentially the same as Murray's answer: treat people with respect and as individuals.[80]

Reich's quotation from a social scientist brings us, finally, to the matter of the integrity of science itself. We have proposed what is an essentially scientific way of thinking for all matters about which data may be

---

78. Reich, *op. cit.*, p. 250.

79. *Op. cit.*, p. 265.

80. Reich, *loc. cit.*

collected. How, it might fairly be asked, is the scientific enterprise itself doing in this respect? The answer is that science is doing quite well… but not perfectly.

. There is, famously, a "replicability crisis" in twenty-first century science.[81]

This replication crisis—that a disturbingly low proportion of scientific research results can be repeated by other, subsequent, researchers—has been worst in the behavioral sciences but has also been seen in the bio-medical sciences, the latter with a replication rate of about 50 percent.[82] The reproducibility rate in psychology published research papers in the cited study was even lower at 39 percent, and, distressingly, the nonrep-licated research results were more likely—much more likely—to be cited by other papers than the replicable results.[83] The latter phenomenon owing, presumably, to the researchers using a lower standard of accep-tance for more theoretically or substantively interesting results.

So thin is the epistemological ice upon which the social sciences find themselves that they have found themselves the butt of a series of hoaxes wherein "authors" have taken social science jargon, mixed it in with dollops of progressive ideology (the received ideology in academic social science) and written articles which were published—*published*—in social science journals. The first of these (of which we are aware) was the famous "Sokal Affair" in which New York University physicist Alan Sokal took a goofy, nonsensical assertion about Einsteinian physics from

81. David Nield, *The 'Replication Crisis' Could be Worse Than We Thought, New Analysis Reveals* (Science Alert: 2021), https://www.sciencealert.com/non-replicable-studies-make-the-most-impact-scientists-find

82. Philip Hunter, The Reproducibility "Crisis:" Reaction to Replication Crisis Should not Stifle Innovation (US National Library of Medicine: 2017), https://www.ncbi.nlm.nih.gov/pmc/articles/PMC5579390/

83. Nield, *op cit.*

Jacques Derrida and just started jamming on it, blending in huge scoops of progressive ideological trope and coming up with an article which was published in *Social Text* in the Spring/Summer 1996 issue.[84]

This was followed—as might have been predicted—by the so-called "Sokal-Squared" affair:

> Over the past 12 months, three scholars—James Lindsay, Helen Pluckrose, and Peter Boghossian—wrote 20 fake papers using fashionable jargon to argue for ridiculous conclusions, and tried to get them placed in high-profile journals in fields including gender studies, queer studies, and fat studies. Their success rate was remarkable: By the time they took their experiment public late on Tuesday, seven of their articles had been accepted for publication by ostensibly serious peer-reviewed journals. Seven more were still going through various stages of the review process. Only six had been rejected.[85]

The reputation of science—the trustworthiness of science—is a problem which needs resolution for science itself ... but also for us. We have proposed an evidence-based way of thinking as a (partial) resolution for the ideological divide in our society. That science itself must be purged of *all* ideological cant goes (almost) without saying. If a scientific way of thinking is going to be relied upon, then it is critical that science itself be trusted. Replicability is key to science and to all evidence-based thinking: it ties everybody to the same reality standard.

---

84. Steven Weinberg, *Sokal's Hoax* (The New York Review of Books: 1996), https://physics.nyu.edu/sokal/weinberg.html

85. Yascha Mounk, *What an Audacious Hoax Reveals About Academia* (The Atlantic: 2018), https://www.theatlantic.com/ideas/archive/2018/10/new-sokal-hoax/572212/

Institutions such as the Center for Open Science provide for the prereg-istration of hypotheses.[86] This is good professional practice and militates against "P-Hacking"—the practice by the researcher of correlating every measured variable with every other measured variable and subjecting the results to, say, a .05 level of statistical significance to generate "find-ings"—and other sorts of mischief.

One may say the same about *any* forensic enterprise. Journalism, how-ever, may be singled out for special mention.

Trump's despicable "enemy of the people" rants notwithstanding, the press is—necessarily—a cognoscenti enterprise. This, by itself, does not mean that our Fourth Estate needs to have a cognoscenti ideological bias, and an informed person may think of counterinstances: even-handed journalism or even a right-wing press. This cognoscenti character of the press, however, underscores the importance of professional, rules-based journalism … not only in how one reports a story but in which stories one chooses to report. A free, professional, and even-handed press—*The People's Intelligence Service*—is absolutely key to a functioning democracy. (There: another bias revealed.)

86. *Registered Reports: Peer Review Before Results are Known to Align Scientific Values and Practices* (Center for Open Science, accessed 2022), https://www.cos.io/initiatives/registered-reports

XII. BELIEVING

> Never play cards with a man called Doc.
> Never eat at a place called Mom's.
> Never sleep with a woman whose troubles are worse than
> your own.
>
> —Nelson Algren

ONE MIGHT BE FORGIVEN FOR coming away from the previous chapter with a reading that the epistemological problem of the yeomanry is ignorance—if a rather studied and self-imposed ignorance—and that the epistemological problem of the cognoscenti is self-deception—if a smugly sanctimonious self-deception. But this would be a misreading of the chapter. In fact, both sectors participate in both sorts of cognitive malpractice, and both are sufficiently deformed that they both may be "triggered" by exposure to a heterodox argument. The ideology of the yeomanry isn't based simply on ignorance—not knowing or believing falsely—it is also inflected by the circumstances of their lives: for example, by generalizing from the parochial circumstances of traditional organization for the resolution of national and international-level problems. And the cognoscenti is not simply self-deluded by its pursuit of ideological fashionability, benighted not simply in—but by virtue of—its progressiveness; it is also steered into ignorance—through confirmation bias and other mechanisms—in areas where evidence conflicts with the demands of fashion.

The most vexing problem elevated by the sociology of knowledge is, of course, the epistemological problem: if one's thought depends upon one's social position, then how can one know if one's belief is ultimately and transcendently (in the sense of transcending specific situations) true? One hastens to say that the fact that a belief derives from a social situation does not, strictly speaking, have any bearing on its truth value: one may, of course, get to a correct conclusion based upon an incorrect predicate.

Moreover, there are large areas of knowledge for which social position has no practical impact upon thinking. In closed logical systems such as mathematics, for instance, or formal logic, once primal assumptions are agreed upon, then conclusions *via* proof follow (excepting for logical error). In addition, within such closed logical systems (and as distinct from the sciences), proven propositions may be said to be literally "true" rather than stochastically probable.

For people who subscribe assiduously to systems of faith, the problem of ultimate truth finds an *a priori* solution in scripture, notwithstanding that there can be variations in the interpretation of scripture which might be susceptible to social influence. The Abrahamic religions, in particular—Judaism, Christianity and Islam—are faith-based ... by contrast with the more wisdom-based religions of the East. These faith traditions are important sources of certainty for believers, though subscribers to all faiths confront enormous difficulty communicating these certainties to those who reside outside their own communities of faith. Diversity comes with costs.

A. THE CASE OF THE SCIENCES

The natural and physical sciences, too, are largely—though not completely—impervious to the influences of society (Obviously, tell that to Galileo.). Moreover, science, as a set of results and theoretical constructs rather than as a method, is never stable. Science, as we have discussed in the last chapter, comes up with the best explanation—the idea which best accounts for—the evidence available at the time. In our view, therefore, the frequently used phrase "settled science" is a misnomer: there is no such thing. Science is a living, moving enterprise. Science produces the best explanation available, not the transcendent Truth. If a science could produce ultimate Truth, that science would cease to be alive; it would have explained everything perfectly; that hasn't happened yet, nor is it likely.

Consider geology in the mid-twentieth century, just prior to the revolution wrought by plate tectonics. Geologists knew that there was some relationship between orogeny—the creation of mountains—and seismic activity, or earthquakes. This gave them a capacity to predict, statistically, where most earthquakes would occur. The theory of orogeny in the early twentieth century was based on the concept of a "geosyncline," a large trough which would fill up with sediment and subsequently (and inexplicably) begin rising thus creating mountains ... with earthquakes being associated with all of the deformation accompanying this orogeny. Comes now plate tectonics! This new theory, based on new data and new thinking, argues that the surface of the Earth is covered by huge, moving, shifting plates of rock. The collision of these moving plates at their margins and the subduction of one beneath the other provides an antecedent cause which can explain *both* orogeny and seismic activity and why they occur in the same locations. Now—and this is the real point of this discussion—would one call those early twentieth-century geologists "wrong" in their thinking? They could base a useful technology of earthquake location prediction upon their scientific thinking; their thinking was better than that of their nineteenth-century counterparts; they produced the best explanation for the evidence available given the level of their theory and data at the time. So, in our view, one wouldn't call them "wrong." And would one call the theories that the plate tectonics geologists produced the "true view?" Geologists still can't adequately explain the rare (10% or so) earthquakes which occur away from the plate margins. So, geology isn't in the Truth business; it's in the "best explanation" business.

Or consider twentieth-century physics. Would one consider Newtonian mechanics "wrong" in light of subsequent Einsteinian Relativity physics? Most engineering calculations are still based on the assumptions of classical Newtonian mechanics. Or would one consider Einsteinian physicists "wrong" during the period after the advent of Quantum mechanics? Again, of course, the answer is "no"; the physicists provided the best explanation of the evidence given what they had in terms of theory and data at the time.

This brief foray into the harder sciences illustrates that they are living enterprises which increase—sometimes slowly, sometimes rapidly—in their explanatory and predictive powers. They are also largely immune from social influence, rear guard actions by certain religious groups objecting to the idea of biological evolution and/or geologic time notwithstanding.

The other point which we would make about science—and a point which may be extended to any forensic discipline like business research or intelligence analysis—is that, even if such disciplines yield only probabilistic conclusions, even if they never yield "settled science" (let alone

"Absolute Truth"), they still provide bases for making decisions; they still yield conclusions which can serve to guide personal action or collective policy.

B. KARL MANNHEIM AND THE EPISTEMOLOGICAL PROBLEM

We have been discussing the so-called "epistemological problem" of the sociology of knowledge. Epistemology is the field of philosophy dealing with the nature and sources of human knowledge. We have said that ideas reflect the position in social organizations which the subscribers and formulators of those ideas occupy. This sociology of knowledge way of thinking is, as a way of thinking about ideas and their sources, a departure from the Western positivistic philosophical tradition in which good ideas are understood to be rooted in valid evidence and/or sound inference and bad ideas in defective evidence and/or incorrect inference. What does the fact that social and economic factors influence the creation and acceptance of ideas say about the truth value of these ideas?

This problem is not, formally speaking, really a problem for the sociology of knowledge at all in that the sociology of knowledge purports to be a "scientific" endeavor whereas its epistemological problem is a philosophical problem: somebody else's business. Still, you make a bit of a mess of things once you say that ideas come from a material, social source, and everybody who visits the sociology of knowledge would like to see it clean up its own mess. To the extent that the sociology of knowledge leads one to make assertions of the form: "You are saying (or thinking) that because you're a _____ [fill in the blank]," is it raising questions about the validity of what "you" are saying? When you ask a faculty member from a university department of literature from New England and a feed store owner from East Cowflop, Missouri, whether there ought to be a federal or state law mandating recognition of same-sex marriages, you are going to get characteristically different answers: characteristic in the important sense that you could ask this question of fifty of each kind of person, and the pattern of answers would characterize and distinguish each group. Clearly, "yes" and "no" cannot both be correct answers to the same question in the usual sense of the term "correct" (i.e., objectively correct, independently of who is giving the answer).

In fact, one could (logically but not, we believe, particularly usefully) turn the sociology of knowledge back on itself and do a sociology of knowledge analysis of the sociology of knowledge. It would go something like this: "The sociology of knowledge is, clearly, a product of its own historic time and place. It could only appear at a time of rapid social change and growing social diversity. Only in such a setting could questions challenging traditional ideas about correctness and error, about the sources and truth value of thought, arise; only under circumstances of all social institutions and traditional beliefs being questioned could such a 'debunking' mentality be thought up and successfully communicated. The sociology of knowledge is, therefore, itself socially (and techno-economically) determined, and so, too, are all of its pronouncements."

Karl Mannheim (1893-1947), a sociologist who worked in the early part of the twentieth century, has done the most widely received analysis of the epistemological problem of the sociology of knowledge. Indeed, Mannheim's work in the sociology of knowledge is central to the field and remains perhaps the most comprehensive consideration of the relationship between social organization and thought. Returning to the specific problem, the epistemological problem, Mannheim begins[87] with

87. Mannheim, *op cit.*, p. 290.

an argument that the criteria for correctness used by the natural and physical sciences are not appropriate for use in the case of social and political knowledge. He follows this with an argument that the criteria for correctness themselves change over time to reflect the changed nature of knowledge in (he is writing prior to publication in 1936) the emerging complex industrial European society of his time.

In traditional epistemology the source of a proposition is held to be irrelevant to its truth value. A person might, for instance, be right but for the wrong reason. Mannheim argues that this version of epistemology must be changed for application to social and political knowledge:

> Indeed, if the type of knowledge represented by the example 2 X 2 = 4 is subjected to examination, then the correctness of this thesis is fairly well demonstrated. It is true of this type of knowledge that its genesis does not enter into the results of thought... . . There are, however, types of genesis which are not void of meaning, the peculiarities of which have until now never been analyzed.... .. A position in the social structure carries with it, as we have seen, the probability that he who occupies it will think in a certain way. It signifies existence oriented with reference to certain meanings (*Sinnausgerichtetes Sein*). Social position cannot be described in terms which are devoid of social meanings as, for example, by mere chronological designation. 1789 as a chronological date is wholly meaningless. As historical designation, however, this date refers to a set of meaningful social events which in themselves demarcate the range of a certain type of experiences, conflicts, attitudes, and thoughts.[88]

---

88. *Ibid.* pp. 293-294.

Well, given that (in Mannheim's view) the criteria for truth might change based on changes in historical condition, is there some general guidance which he can provide as to what constitutes true and valid knowledge which we can use to make decisions for ourselves? He does; in a frequently quoted passage, Mannheim asserts that:

> A theory then is wrong if in a given practical situation it uses concepts and categories which, if taken seriously, would prevent man from adjusting himself in that historical stage.[89]

C. THE IDEA OF "FALSE CONSCIOUSNESS"

The idea of false consciousness comes from Karl Marx and relies on his more fundamental ideas that, first, consciousness reflects the social and economic substructure in which it emerges, and second, that the ruling ideas of any age are the ideas of that age's ruling class. It's clear what Marx means by "ruling class;" what he means by "ruling ideas" are those ideas accepted as being non-problematic by the masses of people, the general public. A bit more specifically, he is talking about ideas that derive from the existing relations of production and which *support* these relations of production and not about popularly shared ideas about empirically verifiable matters (e.g., the popularly shared idea that the sun rises in the east [due to the rotation of the Earth] in the morning or which direction of rotation is "clockwise").

What Marx means by "false consciousness" is not specifically that the ideas in the peoples' consciousness are wrong (though false consciousness generally leads to wrong ideas). It doesn't even mean that the peoples' thought processes lead to incorrect ideas. What he really

---

89. *Ibid.*, p. 95.

means is that the masses of people don't understand that ideas about social arrangements are socially determined and are mediated to them by their rulers and used on behalf of these rulers to maintain their rule. For Marx, then, dispelling false consciousness is a matter of learning his own version of the sociology of knowledge!

And that's something like what we mean, too, though in our view *false consciousness arises not only from exogenous sources—false ideas mediated to people from outside of their own sector—but also from endogenous false ideas: distortions of thought which arise from the ideological forces playing upon the individual by virtue of his or her incumbency in their own sector.* "False," in both of these cases, means demonstrably false: that a reasonable thinker can demonstrate that data exist which can honestly falsify the idea; accordingly, the exorcism of such false consciousness is limited to matters about which data may be collected. The endogenous forces—the ideological themes typical to the cognoscenti and the yeomanry—were discussed in Chapters VII and VIII respectively, and the way in which these ideological tropes distort the thinking of their subscribers was discussed in Chapter XI. In this section we will be discussing the former basis of false consciousness: exogenous ideas.

We have argued above that there are two important sectors in American society: the yeomanry and the cognoscenti. We have argued, further, that these two sectors generate different and conflicting ideologies and that the sectors themselves consist of the populations which staff different industrial sectors and which support certain appurtenant (ideological constituency) groups. Finally, we have argued that the ideologies produced by the sectors are promulgated to the wider society and fortify the positions of these sectors in the society. They do this based, first, on their control of and access to the institutions by which culture is produced, and, second, on their control of or access to the media through which culture is transmitted ... and we have said that the cognoscenti sector is, in general, better at this than is the yeomanry sector because the formal organizations supporting these specific institutions are a pivotally important part of the cognoscenti social base. A third factor in this control of ideas is the capacity to define: the capacity—which great social and economic power confers—to label ideas "fashionable" or otherwise acceptable or desirable.

The fact that these ideas come from somebody else—somebody powerful—does not, by itself, mean that the ideas are incorrect or contrary to one's own interests or corrosive of one's family's or group's culture, but this fact ought to make the prudent person pause and exercise conscious judgment regarding the acceptability of these ideas. In sociological phrasing, this would mean questioning the authority of the sources of these ideas or "delegitimating" them. An authoritative idea is one you accept without questioning because you accept as legitimate the power of the source of that idea.

It is one of the personal implications of this book that the social ideas being mediated to us from ideological sources ought to be questioned ... questioned in matters of factual correctness, questioned in their internal logic, and questioned with respect to their comprehension of and compatibility with the interests and positions of you and the people you care about. One looks, but looks in vain, for a universally "honest broker," an impartial and informed party which could support popular decision-making by summoning evidence and expertise on behalf of the masses of people. Social science ought to be able to serve this role, but social science—and sociology, in particular—has been utterly co-opted by the cognoscenti Left.[90] This is a great dark sadness, the only

---

90. This state of affairs in twentieth century American sociology has been addressed in detail by Irving Louis Horowitz, *The Decomposition of Sociology* (New York: Oxford University Press, 1994).

mitigating beam of light in which is the unadorned obviousness of this co-optation. In fact, as we have said, the work experience of social scientists virtually determines that they will end up on the Left side of things. Consider (again) what a social scientist does for a living: he or she is supposed to come up with rational models for human behavior, to apply (when they're at their best) reason to the world of people and their groups and beliefs. Now, this is not at all the way that most of humanity regards people and their groups and beliefs! For most people these objects are, above all others, invested with morality and meaning ... they are the last things about which you'd be coolly analytical. This rational and manipulating style—which comes with the occupational territory— powerfully predisposes social scientists to be secular and view the social world as malleable and manipulable. This style is fine by itself, but, in the contemporary American social context, it virtually ordains that social scientists will fall into orbit around the cognoscenti. Add to this the "leftish" character of universities generally and the role played by social science in bolstering government social service provision programs, and the ideological position of social scientists can only be regarded as being overdetermined.

We are, then, left on our own to base our views on the best evidence which we can summon—from scientists, honest journalists[91] and other uncompromised sources of information—and upon the best thinking which we as thinking beings can bring to bear on these decisions. We must also proceed into these decisions with a candid view of our own material interests and pre-existing perspectives, because nobody outside

---

91. We might say, as a matter of editorial opinion, that—for all of the condemnation of the "liberal press," and some evidence that individual journalists are ideologically more canted to the Left than to the Right (as our theory says they ought to be)—we find that the press does a better job of presenting ideologically-infused issues fairly than do social scientists, politicians, or hired ideological guns from the law firms, public relations firms, etc.

of our own groups is going to do that for us; indeed, everybody else with a reasonable crack at the microphone has their own—or their clients'—agendas in mind. We may be awash and alone, but we need not drown if we know how to swim.

The consequences of false consciousness are to a great extent obvious once the process is understood: the process we have described in the foregoing chapters by which ideas of other groups with agendas other than your own are developed, transmitted, ornamented with moralization, and delivered to you as morally obligatory or fashionable ideology.

At the level of the thinking of the individual, the consequences are two-fold. First, one is presented with ideas reflecting the interests and real perspectives of other groups—groups with interests and real perspectives which may be (and, in reality, often are) discrepant with one's own—packaged together with an appeal to "principles" or "values" also supportive of these group interests and perspectives and subscription to which is required—under penalty of being labeled as being immoral or unfashionable—not only in one's public utterances but in the privacy of one's own heart and mind. Thus, one is compelled by false consciousness into positions destructive to the interests (whether material or conceptual) of oneself and one's family and the interests of people who share a similar position in the world.

Second, to fail to understand how the process of ideological formation in American life operates is just that: a failure. And to understand is always better than to not understand.

At the level of policy—a level at which, presumably, human intelligence is applied to the social world—the consequences of false consciousness are simply an extension of the problems at the individual level. Important policy topics remain undiscussed or underdiscussed because inappropriate moralization turns these topics from matters of evidence and reason to matters of faith, and the faiths available are governed by the orthodoxy of some party's version of a received ideology.

Thomas Frank—naming his native state in the title of his book—posed the question, "What's the Matter with Kansas?"[92] The problem with Kansans being, presumably, that they believed and believe things that are materially bad for them. It's a fair question—and certainly a question which goes to the issue of false consciousness—but one might, with as much justification, ask the question "What's the Matter with Manhattan?" (And we don't mean Manhattan, Kansas.). There are plenty of people in that bubble, too, who believe things which are bad for themselves and for their loved ones.

D. THOUGHTS ON MAKING GOOD DECISIONS

The literature of decision-making is, by now, extremely sophisticated and quite voluminous. Scholars such as Philip Tetlock[93] have turned this area into a science—certainly a technology—in its own right. We intend here to make only topically specific and glancing blow at this major issue arena.

We have noted above the frequently quoted passage from Mannheim asserting that:

> A theory then is wrong if in a given practical situation it uses concepts and categories which, if taken seriously, would prevent man from adjusting himself in that historical stage.[94]

Mannheim's point should probably be taken as good advice.

---

92. Thomas Frank, *What's the Matter with Kansas?* (New York: Henry Holt & Co., 2004).

93. *Philip E. Tetlock* (University of Pennsylvania: accessed 2022), https://www.sas.upenn.edu/tetlock/

94. Mannheim, *op. cit.,* p. 95.

Nonetheless, it is advice which has been stridently criticized by some on the grounds that it is "conservative" or "utilitarian:" stated another way, Mannheim's advice is criticized on the grounds that he is asserting that one ought to reject theories—and the concepts and categories on which they are based—if these items of thought prevent you from adjusting yourself to life. By now—and if you've accepted the arguments advanced in this book—you should be telling yourself that this kind of criticism isn't just coming in randomly from out of the ozone. It may be coming from the cognoscenti Left, and, of course, you understand by now that by "Left" we don't just mean a philosophical position, we mean a social structural location and people in it who have agendas for themselves and for their constituents.

Or tendentious nonsense might be peddled to you from the Right. The issue of urban sprawl is, for example, such a topic, where a full, free, and rational public consideration of the matter is powerfully impeded by the copious quantities of "property rights," "growth as a virtue" and "freedom to" ideological tropes ladled onto the issue by interested parties and accepted by people who ought to know better … that is, who ought to know better than to accept as a matter of faith something which is tractable by reason and evidence.

"Values" that lead you to make bad choices are probably bad values.

If you are one of the people in these elite social positions—or one of their constituents—then maybe Mannheim's advice is bad for you. If not, then the advice is probably good for you: you should be receptive to ideas which are reasoned, evidenced, and make sense of the world from your own perspective—including, as components of this perspective, your own experience and interests—*while understanding that your own cognitive perspective is refracted by your own social position.*

Of course, this does not mean that you always and only decide by looking at your own interests. Moral action is always going to proceed with reference to higher and more general bodies of thought—bodies of thought which transcend, in their own history and purview, the here and now—bodies of thought that address matters about which data is not available. These are, in general, metaphysical or religious bodies of thought ... "religious" to be understood to include the wisdom-based traditions of Asia such as Hinduism, Confucianism, Shintoism, and Buddhism as well as the monotheistic faith-based traditions originating at the eastern end of the Mediterranean: Christianity, Judaism and Islam (And, of course, others; all groups have—or once had—a faith of their fathers.). Such bodies of thought share the advantages of having transcended not only the "here" but also the "now." These philosophical systems incorporate millennia of human experience as transcribed by the most inspired humans contemporaneously available. Their wisdom has been won by the inclusion—over the scores of centuries—of ideas derived from the interaction between conscious, intelligent human beings and the circumstances in which they have found themselves over those many years, precisely the kind of interaction, which is explicit in Mannheim's dictum, though generalized over the centuries. This sort of adaptation of human life to reality gradually and over the millennia—and its interpretation by the most thoughtful and inspired people of their respective times—is precious stuff and the best guide available to us for moral and ethical moderation of self-interested and parochially inflected behavior. That these traditions should occupy a position of such low salience and esteem in our popular culture—that they should be routinely derogated in that popular culture—should stand in testimony to the quality and character of the nation's popular culture. What's different now is that you should understand why—and on whose behalf—such derogation occurs.

One powerful test of whether a belief such as a moral principle is one which transcends a particular situation is whether such a belief is extensive over *either* time or space or—optimally—*both*. In other words, is the belief of long historical venerability or is the belief of wide cross-cultural extent, or both? For example, the Golden Rule exists in all major religions—Eastern and Western—*and* has had expression in all of these faiths for a very long time.[95] Christians know the Golden Rule principally from the gospels of Luke and Matthew, but Jesus—by all accounts a very good student of the Tanakh—would simply have been echoing Leviticus 19:18: "Love your neighbor as yourself: I am the Lord."

There is a reasonable argument that such thinking—looking for guidance in what has worked for humankind across time and across space—is, by definition, conservative. That's a fair observation; it's not much of a criticism. All we have are time and space ... plus, of course, ideology.

Evidence itself is inherently conservative inasmuch as all of it happened in the past: there is no evidence to be drawn from what hasn't yet happened. If you're going to engage in evidence-based thought, you are necessarily going to be looking to the past—sometimes the recent past, but the past—for guidance.

Now, the power of religious traditions lies, for our purposes, not in their specifically religious, their theological, content but in their "pan-historicity," their demonstrated capacity for having guided human life for millennia. This is not to derogate or deny in any way their religiously transcendent content; however, that's their business; we are looking at them here purely as sources of worldly guidance, and we are interested in their transcendence of time, place, and circumstance, not in some universal theological transcendence. Indeed, the Shintoist and Confucian

---

95. *The Golden Rule* (Religious Naturalism: accessed 2022), https://religiousnaturalism.org/the-golden-rule/

traditions are, relatively speaking, theologically rather secular.

There are other more secular candidates, but they have either tended to come a cropper on the shoals of recent history or are too new and limited in philosophical bailiwick to serve in this guiding capacity. Marxism is one such example. For many Marxists the philosophy of Marxism (which we might date from about 1850) satisfied the requirements of a religion: it provided an ethical structure, a theory of history, a set of guiding principles for behavior, and an eschatology—a theory of the Last Days—in which the proletariat would emerge victorious and the dialectic would end.

Revolutionary Marxism is a failed prophesy. As of 1991 perhaps ten thousand books had been written about the transition from capitalism to communism. No books had been written about the transition from communism to capitalism, and the new Russian Republic has had to make things up as it went along over the course of the past thirty years (and hasn't done it particularly well). Heaven knows, there are still plenty of Marxists out there who think that this is just a temporary setback—a hiccup in the dialectical process—and that one day the Revolutionary Proletariat will emerge victorious ... but there are plenty of people out there, too, who think that the world is going to end on a foreseeable upcoming date, and we shouldn't take them very seriously (either).

Worship of nature—we shall call it Animism—is the most venerable and traditional of all transcendent belief systems. It is a belief that (in the very most general sense) all objects are spiritually inhabited. Animism would certainly help address the anthropogenic destruction of nature that we see all about us. However, that very feature becomes a bug when applying Animism in an overpopulated world ... a bug at least for those imbued with the traditions of Judeo-Christian humanism. How does one behave in a humane manner toward humans when humans—in their present numbers—are the principal destroyers of nature?

Other bodies of thought are either too recent and, for the present at least, too restricted in purview to serve as a guiding philosophy for broad swaths of human life and experience. Evolution is, for some, another candidate body of thought: it is the best explanation available for the origins and character of life, and it can, in the sociobiological approach to societies, be used to account for features of social organization at various points—including the human point—on the phylogenetic scale. It has about the same time of birth as Marxism. It can even be extended—through some sort of "Social Darwinist" approach—into the sphere of ethics and morality. It has no intellectually serious competitors in the sphere of biological thought. But evolution, as a transcendent idea, is not transcendent enough: it is, for one thing, still too new and too restricted to specifically biological phenomena to provide a viable moral philosophy, and its various forays into human ethical behavior (particularly Social Darwinism) have produced, because of the harshness of their implications, a broadly based rejection.

Making good decisions about matters of ultimate worth and reality must rest on faith. Faith isn't not knowing. Faith is a different way of knowing which one uses in cases which are simply not tractable by evidence. The resources available in these cases are reason, one's belief system about empirically transcendent reality, and one's conscience.

Making good decisions about matters of simple or complex fact ought to rely purely on reason and evidence and on doing the sometimes-hard work necessary to summon the evidence and clear inference needed to make a good decision given the consequences, in a particular case, of making a bad one (you never have perfect information, but you'd work a lot harder, for example, at gathering information about whether to take a new job than about where to go for lunch). In fact, behavioral economist

Daniel Kahneman (based on work with his collaborator Amos Tversky) has developed a useful dichotomous taxonomy of human thinking:[96]

System 1 Thinking. This thinking operates quickly and automatically with little or no deliberation. Say you're driving your car to work. The thinking that governs your driving is System 1 thinking. The guy in front of you hits his brakes: you hit your brakes. You want to change lanes: you glance at your mirrors. Fast, System 1 thinking is necessary for driving. So, you're driving along, thinking, "I hate this commute! I need to move closer to work! There's a house for sale! I'll buy that one!" Hold it right there, pal; driving is one thing; buying a house requires some ...

System 2 Thinking. This thinking is slow, highly deliberative, and based on copious evidence, even if gathering that evidence requires some effort, some cost. Buying a house requires this kind of thinking. It involves decisions about finance, career plans, school zones, on and on.

The sort of discipline brought to thinking by Kahneman's distinction between Systems 1 and 2 thinking would be a good set of habits to bring to anybody's thinking.

Making good decisions about social and political matters is what we are talking about now, and one of the applicable resources is the view of the structure of things which has been presented in the foregoing chapters. It's only one of the resources: the others are the best information and clearest thinking you can reasonably summon and the belief system which you bring to the decision. The gathering of information is your own business; we can only tell you that getting informed can be real work (but you already knew that). Herbert Simon's distinction between "Maximizing" and "Satisficing" (accumulating a data set which is "good

---

96. Daniel Kahneman, *Thinking Fast and Slow* (New York: Farrar, Straus and Giroux, 2011).

enough" even if it's not *all* the data) will be relevant for considering such matters.[97]

A person's life experience is, in sum, a composite of only two things: one's luck—those events and circumstances over which one has, by definition, no control—and one's decisions. Thus, the quality of one's decisions is a good metric for how well a man or a woman has created, has actualized, his or her life. It's worth the effort.

* * * * *

Life is a gamble with terrible odds; if it was a bet you
wouldn't take it.

—Tom Stoppard, *Rosencrantz and Guildenstern Are Dead*

Life, as we teach our children, confronts us with opportunities to make both Little Mistakes and Big Mistakes. The difference between the two is that Little Mistakes are easy and cheap to remedy; Big Mistakes are expensive or impossible to remedy. The capacity to distinguish the two in advance is an important part of that habit of mind we call "judgment." The United States finds itself at a point in history at which it is being given abundant opportunity to make Big Mistakes: the climate crisis, the rise of China as an adversary, a newly-resurrected threat of nuclear war from Russia, the potential for a renegade AI, overpopulation … these— and others—may afford just one chance (if that) for getting it right. If the United States is to remain the planet's preeminent stalwart for liberal democracy—as it should—we'll need to make our best national decisions as we engage these great issues. We'll need to do our best thinking. We hope that this volume has been a contribution to good thinking. And

97. Herbert A. Simon, *Administrative Behavior: A Study of Decision-Making Processes in Administrative Organization* (New York: McMillan, 1947).

we'll need to stand shoulder-to-shoulder together—as we have in the past—our diversity and our divisions notwithstanding. It may not—it will not—be completely comfortable. But, then, it never was.

So, be kind—yeomanry and cognoscenti—and good luck.